ISBN: 9781290936262

Published by:
HardPress Publishing
8345 NW 66TH ST #2561
MIAMI FL 33166-2626

Email: info@hardpress.net
Web: http://www.hardpress.net

ON THE ART OF THE THEATRE

THE MASQUE OF LONDON. WAPPING OLD STAIRS

Quite an impossible scene; that is to say, impossible to realize on a stage. But I wanted to know for once what it felt like to be mounting up impossible ladders and beckoning to people to come up after me.

ON THE ART OF THE THEATRE

BY EDWARD GORDON CRAIG

BROWNE'S BOOKSTORE
CHICAGO

First printed December 1911
Second Impression January 1912

Printed in England.

TO THE EVER LIVING GENIUS
OF THE GREATEST OF ENGLISH ARTISTS
WILLIAM BLAKE
AND TO THE ILLUSTRIOUS MEMORY
OF HIS WIFE
THIS BOOK IS DEDICATED

PREFACE

WHAT should be said as Preface? Should one ask for forgiveness from those one unwittingly offends? Should one admit that words are all nonsense, and that theories, even after one has practised that about which one theorizes, are really of little account? Or should one stand on the threshold and receive one's guests and hope that they will enjoy themselves? I think I shall do the latter.

Well, in this case, my guests are made up of a thousand invited friends and those half-dozen one did not invite and never would invite, because of their very evil or foolish intentions towards our art. For instance, I willingly throw open the doors of this book to my very dear friends the artists, whether they be painters, sculptors, musicians, poets or architects. These, of course, will stand aside for a moment to allow first of all the beautiful ladies to pass. Then there are the scholars. Well, as I have only schooled myself in one particular branch of knowledge, I feel very shy about meeting such guests.

Coming after them is that group of kindly people, men and women, who, without knowing much about art, are fond of it and encourage its growth. These, I am happy to believe, will feel at home here.

Then there are other surprises, those engineers, those directors of journals, those managers of stores, those sea captains, men who startle one by suddenly putting in an appearance and expressing a sincere and hearty desire to join in the festivities.

Last of all, there is what is known as the theatrical profession. How many of these will accept my invitation? A rare few, perhaps, but certainly the best.

So, when the rest of us have all assembled, we shall welcome Hevesi, from Budapest; Stanislawski, Sulergitski, Mosquin, and Katchalof, who come from Moscow; Meyerkhold, who comes from St. Petersburg; De Vos, from Amsterdam; Starke, from Frankfurt; Fuchs, from Munich; Antoine, Paul Fort and Madame Guilbert, from Paris; and our great poet who has won over the stage, Yeats, from Ireland; and after these the shades of Vallentin, from Berlin; Wyspiansky, from Krakow; and Appia from Italy.

Least of all are the uninvited guests, with their cheap cynicism and witty remarks which are calculated to put a blight upon every pleasant moment, upon every achievement, who will attempt to rob our happy gathering of all enjoyment, if they can possibly do so.

Well, let us hope for the best, that these people will stay away. To the others I present what is within the house and beg that they will forever hold towards it and myself good thoughts.

Being in my own house, I let myself go. I am not careful to be cautious among my friends. If I were to do so, they would think that I suspected them of being spies.

It is a great honour for me to feel that among my friends are the names of the first artists in Europe. And I think we can all feel happy on the progress which our movement has made, a movement which is destined ultimately to restore the Art of the Theatre into its ancient position among the Fine Arts.

E. G. C

London, 1911.

CONTENTS

ILLUSTRATIONS

By EDWARD GORDON CRAIG

SELECTED FROM HIS COLLECTION OF DESIGNS FOR STAGE SCENES AND COSTUMES

INTRODUCTION

I THINK Mr. Craig is the truest revolutionist I have ever known, because he demands a return to the most ancient traditions of which we can dream. Revolution and revelation are not far each from the other, and he gives us both. His torch, destined to set on fire our pseudo-Theatres, our monstrous and barbarous play-houses, has been kindled at the sacred fires of the most ancient arts. He discovered for us that in a rope-dancer there may be more theatrical art than in an up-to-date actor reciting from his memory and depending on his prompter. I am sure all who are working on the stage throughout Europe, creative minds, or stage-managers priding themselves on their being creative minds, cannot be but most grateful to Mr. Craig, and must regard all that is and shall be done in his honour to be done in the vital interest of the very Art of the Theatre.

For more than a hundred years there have been two men working on the stage, spoiling almost all that is to be called Theatrical Art. These two men are the Realist and the Machinist. The Realist offers imitation for life, and the Machinist tricks in place of marvels. So we have lost the truth and the marvel of life—that is, we have lost the main thing possessed by the art. The Art of the Theatre as pure imitation is nothing but an alarming demonstration of the abundance of life and the narrowness of Art.

It is like the ancient example of the child who was trying to empty the sea with a shell, and, as for the wonderful tricks of the machinist, they may be marvellous, but they can never be a marvel. A flying machine is marvellous, but a bird is *a marvel.*

To the true Artist common life is a marvel and Art more abundant, more intense and more living than life itself. True Art is always discovering the marvel in all that does not seem to be marvellous at all, because Art is not imitation, but vision.

That is the great discovery of Mr. Craig on the stage. He found the forgotten wonderland with the sleeping beauty, the land of our dreams and wishes, and has fought for it with the gestures of an artist, with the soul of a child, with the knowledge of a student, and with the constancy of a lover. He has done the greatest service to the Art in which we are so profoundly interested, and it is a great happiness for us all that he comes off with flying colours.

He has his admirers and followers in our little Hungary, the whole of the new generation being under his influence, and, without any disparagement to the great merit and good luck of Prof. Reinhardt, we Hungarians, as close neighbours and good observers, dare say that almost all that has been done in Berlin and Dusseldorf, in Munich or in Manheim for the last ten years is to be called the success of Mr. Craig.

I am very sorry that I am not able to express all that I feel in a better style. But I am writing in a language which is not mine, and, living in a country cottage, far even from my English dictionaries, I am obliged to write it as I can, and not as I would.

July 10, 1911.

DR. ALEXANDER HEVESI,

Dramaturg-Regisseur of the State Theatre, Budapest

ELECTRA. SOPHOCLES

A vast and forbidding doorway, I often think, still remains the best background for any tragedy—yet when I am told by the archæologist, who enjoys himself in the dry and dusty days which are gone, that vastness and nobility of line are unimportant, and that a nice little wooden stage and some tasteful hangings about eight to ten feet high will serve, I am so ready to agree that I sometimes wonder whether these vast doors and open spaces, these shadows and these bursts of light are not out of place.

Of course, it all depends whether you come to the theatre for drama or literature.

If you come for drama, then let the whole thing live—not alone to the brain, but through the eye and the ear.

If you come for a literary treat—best catch the first train home and own up to having made a blunder.

ELECTRA. SOPHOCLES

A vast and forbidding doorway, I often think, still remains the best background for any tragedy—yet when I am told by the archaeologist, who enjoys himself in the dry and dusty days which are gone, that vastness and nobility of line are unimportant, and that a nice little wooden stage and some tasteful hangings about eight to ten feet high will serve, I am so ready to agree that I sometimes wonder whether these vast doors and open spaces, these shadows and these bursts of light are not out of place.

Of course, it all depends whether you come to the theatre for drama or literature.

If you come for drama, then let the whole thing live—not alone to the brain, but through the eye and the ear.

If you come for a literary treat—best catch the first train home and own up to having made a blunder.

[Face page xiv.

GOD SAVE THE KING

"It is meritorious to insist on forms. Religion and all else naturally clothes itself in forms. All substances clothe themselves in forms; but there are suitable true forms, and then there are untrue unsuitable. As the briefest definition one might say, Forms which GROW round a substance, if we rightly understand that, will correspond to the real Nature and purport of it, will be true, good; forms which are consciously *put* round a substance, bad. I invite you to reflect on this. It distinguishes true from false in Ceremonial Form, earnest solemnity from empty pageant, in all human things."—CARLYLE.

I SPEAK here as the Artist, and though all artists labour and most are poor, all are loyal, all are the worshippers of Royalty. If there is a thing in the world that I love it is a symbol.

If there is a symbol of heaven that I can bend my knee to it is the sky, if there is a symbol of God, the Sun. As for the smaller things which I can touch I am not content to believe in them, as though they could ever be *the* thing. This I must always keep as something precious. All I ask is that I may be allowed to see it, and what I see must be superb. Therefore God save the King!

"All Architecture is what you do to it when you look upon it."[1] So do we artists feel about Royalty, and see it more splendid and more noble than any others can ever see it. And if my King wanted to chop off my head I think I would submit cheerfully and dance to the block for the sake of preserving my ideal of Kingship.

Kings have given us everything, and we in times gone by have in return made up the splendid procession which follows in their wake. Kings have not stopped giving us everything, but we, alas, have

[1] Whitman.

lately given up forming the splendid processions. We have lost the trick of it because we are losing the old power of our eyes and our other senses. Our senses—those wonderful servants of ours over whom *we* reign as king—our senses have rebelled. So that it comes to this: that we on our part have lost our royalty. Our senses have had the vanity and the impertinence to revolt. This is infinitely disgusting. Our senses, if you please, are permitting themselves the luxury of becoming tired. They want another ruler than the Soul, and expect Jupiter to send them a better. We have pampered our intellect so much of late, have searched the archives of knowledge at so great an expense, that we have bargained our senses away to our unimaginative reason.

It costs all this to become practical to-day; our imagination is the price we pay, a pretty penny indeed. It seems that in the Garden of Paradise, the world, there are as many trees of knowledge as there are men, so that it will no longer do to put our continual yearly "fall" down to woman, and we had surely better try to support her bitter laughter than that harsher scorn of the gods.

And the gods *are* laughing! My God, so entirely peerless, laughs only with his eyes. He laughs on all the day, and I hear the echo of his laughter all the night. But I know how nobly all has been arranged in this Garden, for my God's laughter is as the song of Paradise in my ears, and its pale echo soothes me to sleep through the night.

And as surely as this bounteous laughter pours down on me by day and flows away from me by night, so will I find some way of giving thanks for it all: thanksgiving to the joyous laughter and the Royal comfort that it brings.

But to many ears this laughter of the Gods is like the shrieking of a storm, and these people raise their eyebrows, grumble, and pray that it will pass.

But *will* it pass? Will it not shriek in their ears until they be dead, until they have lost the sense of hearing?

Better would it be for these beings to value once more their most noble servants the senses, and attempt to perceive by their means the full meaning of the voice and of the face of God. And when they have understood that they will see the full meaning of the King.

While I worship the sun I cannot listen to the talk which twaddles on about the tyranny of kings. The Sun is for me the greatest of tyrants; that, in fact, is part of my reason for loving the Sun.

All truth, the truth of tyranny no less than the truth of slavery, is illumined by the Sun. From the marble columns of Mount Carrara to the wrinkle on the face of my nurse, all is laid bare for me and illumined by his light; nothing escapes the eye of God. He is a terrible God to those who fear to be burnt by him. From these he will "breed maggots."

The Beautiful and the Terrible. Which is which will never be put into words. But I am free to tell myself; and, let me but preserve the senses—my eyes, my ears, my touch, and all shall be well—all shall seem far more beautiful than terrible.

For not only do these servants of our Royalty help to idealize all things for us, but they also help to fix a limit to our vanity. By their help

I recognize my God as he rises like the spirit of Imagination from the East and sails across the blue straits of heaven.

If I had lost the sense of sight I should be unable to see this glory, and, not seeing it, I should demand other miracles from it than Happiness may expect. I should look for it to work some practical daily miracle in vain. Whereas, seeing this daily glory, this Sun, I know that the miracle *comes and goes*, that the miracle is just the *passage* of this symbol of the Divine, this seeming motion of the Sun from east to west.

And that seeming motion of this God is enough for man to know. Mystic voices seem to cry, " Seek to know no more "; and we answer rebelliously, " I will be satisfied; deny me this and an eternal curse fall on ye."

> "Show his eyes and grieve his heart,
> Come like shadows, so depart."

This seeking to know more—this desire of the brain—threatens to rob our senses of their vitality; our eyes may become dim till we shall no longer recognize the God before us, nor the King as he passes along our way. Our ears seem to be deaf; we begin not to hear the song of Paradise, we fail to pick up the chorus which follows in the wake of Royalty. Our touch, too, is growing coarse. The hem of the robes' brocade was once pleasant to our fingers' touch; to touch the silken glove with our lips was once a privilege and a luxury. Now we have become the mob; ambition's aim, oh noble consummation! Afraid any longer to serve like noblemen, we must slave like thieves, having robbed ourselves of our greatest possession, our fine senses.

We are becoming veritable slaves chained together by circumstances, refusing daily to be released by our imagination, that only power which achieves true Freedom.

But for me. I am a free man, by the grace of Royalty. Long live the King!

E. G. C.

Florence, 1911.

THE ARTISTS OF THE THEATRE OF THE FUTURE

DEDICATED TO THE YOUNG RACE OF ATHLETIC WORKERS IN ALL THE THEATRES.

SECOND THOUGHTS. I DEDICATE THIS TO THE SINGLE COURAGEOUS INDIVIDUALITY IN THE WORLD OF THE THEATRE WHO WILL SOME DAY MASTER AND REMOULD IT.

THEY say that second thoughts are best. They also say it is good to make the best of a bad job, and it is merely making the best of a bad job that I am forced to alter my first and more optimistic dedication to my second. Therefore the second thoughts *are* best. What a pity and what a pain to me that we should be obliged to admit it! No such race of athletic workers in the Theatre of to-day exists; degeneration, both physical and mental, is round us. How could it be otherwise? Perhaps no surer sign of it can be pointed to than that all those whose work lies in the Theatre are to be continually heard announcing that all is well and that the Theatre is to-day at its highest point of development.

But if all were well, no desire for a change would spring up instinctively and continually as it ever does in those who visit or ponder on the modern Theatre. It is because the Theatre is in this wretched state that it becomes necessary that some one shall speak as I do; and then I look around me for those to whom I can speak and for those who will listen and, listening, understand; and I see nothing but backs turned towards me, the backs of a race of unathletic workers. Still the individual, the boy or man of personal courage, faces me. Him I see, and in him I see the force which shall create the race to come. Therefore to him I speak, and I am content that he alone shall understand me. It is the man who will, as Blake says, "leave father, mother, houses and lands if they stand in the way of his art"; it is the man who will give up personal ambition and the temporary success of the moment, he who will cease to desire an agreeable wealth of smooth guineas, but who shall demand as his reward nothing less than the restoration of his home, its liberty, its health, its power. It is to him I speak.

YOU are a young man; you have already been a few years in a theatre, or you have been born of theatrical parents; or you have been a painter for a while but have felt the longing towards movement; or you have been a manufacturer. Perhaps you quarrelled with your parents when you were eighteen, because you wished to go on the stage, and they would not let you. They perhaps asked why you wanted to go on the stage, and you could give no reasonable answer because you wanted to do that which no reasonable answer could explain; in other words, you wanted to fly. And had you said to your parents, "I want to fly," I think that you would have probably got further than had you alarmed them with the terrible words, "I want to go on the stage."

Millions of such men have had the same desire, this desire for movement, this desire to fly, this desire to be merged in some other creature's being, and not knowing that it was the desire to live in the imagination, some have answered their parents, "I want to be an actor; I want to go on the stage."

It is not that which they want; and the tragedy begins. I think when walking, disturbed with this newly awakened feeling, a young man will say, "*perhaps* I want to be an actor"; and it is only when in the presence of the irate parents that in his desperation he turns the "perhaps" into the definite "I want."

This is probably your case. You want to fly; you want to exist in some other state, to be intoxicated with the air, and to create this state in others.

Try and get out of your head now that you really want "to go on the stage." If, unfortunately, you are upon the stage, try and get out of your head then that you want to be an actor and that it is the end of all your desires. Let us say that you are already an actor; you have been so for four or five years, and already some strange doubt has crept upon you. You will not admit it to any one; your parents would apparently seem to have been right; you will not admit it to yourself, for you have nothing else but this one thing to cheer yourself with. But I'm going to give you all sorts of things to cheer yourself with, and you may with courage and complete good spirits throw what you will to the winds and yet lose nothing of that which you stood up for in the beginning. You may remain on, yet be above the stage.

I shall give you the value of my experience for what it is worth, and may be it will be of some use to you. I shall try to sift what is important for us from what is unimportant; and if while I am telling you all this you want any doubts cleared or any more exact explanations or details, you have only to ask me for them and I am ready to serve you.

To begin with, you have accepted an engagement from the manager of the Theatre. You must serve him faithfully, not because he is paying you a salary, but because you are working under him. And with this obedience to your manager comes the first and the greatest temptation which you will encounter in your whole work.

Because you must not merely obey his words but his wishes; and yet you must not lose yourself. I do not mean to say you must not lose your personality, because it is probable your personality has not come to its complete form. But you must not lose sight of that which you are in quest of, you must not lose the first feeling which possessed you when you seemed to yourself to be in movement with a sense of swinging upwards.

While serving your apprenticeship under your first manager listen to all he has to say and all he can show you about the theatre, about acting, and go further for yourself and search out that which he does not show you. Go where they are painting the scenes; go where they are twisting the electric wires for the lamps; go beneath the stage and look at the elaborate constructions; go up over the stage and ask for information about the ropes and the wheels; but while you are learning all this about the Theatre and about acting be very careful to remember that outside the world of the Theatre you will find greater inspiration than inside it: I mean in nature. The other sources of inspiration are music and architecture.

I tell you to do this because you will not have it told you by your manager. In the Theatre they study from the Theatre. They take the Theatre as their source of inspiration, and if at times some actors go to nature for assistance, it is to one part of nature only, to that which manifests itself in the human being.

This was not so with Henry Irving, but I cannot stop here to tell you of him, for it would mean letter upon letter to put the thing clearly before you. But you can remember that as actor he was unfailingly right, and that he studied all nature in order to find symbols for the expression of his thoughts.

You will be probably told that this man, whom I hold up to you as a peerless actor, did such and such a thing in such and such a way; and you will doubt my counsel; but with all respect to your present manager you must be very careful how much credence you give to what he says and to what he shows, for it is upon such tradition that the Theatre has existed and has degenerated.

What Henry Irving did is one thing; what they tell you he did is another. I have had some experience of this. I played in the same Theatre as Irving in Macbeth, and later on I had the opportunity of playing Macbeth myself in a theatre in the north or the south of England. I was curious to know how much would strike a capable and reliable actor of the usual fifteen years' experience, especially one who was an enthusiastic admirer of Henry Irving. I therefore asked him to be good enough to show me how Irving had treated this or that passage; what he had done and what impression he had created, because it had slipped my memory. The competent actor thereupon revealed to my amazed intelligence something so banal, so clumsy, and so lacking in distinction, that I began to understand how much value was in tradition; and I have had several such experiences.

I have been shown by a competent and worthy actress how Mrs. Siddons played Lady Macbeth.

She would move to the centre of the stage and would begin to make certain movements and certain exclamations which she believed to be a reproduction of what Mrs. Siddons had done. I presume she had received these from some one who had seen Mrs. Siddons. The things which she showed me were utterly worthless in so far as they had no unity, although one action here, another action there, would have some kind of reflected value; and so I began to see the uselessness of this kind of tuition; and it being my nature to rebel against those who would force upon me something which seemed to me unintelligent, I would have nothing to do with such teaching.

I do not recommend you to do the same, although you will disregard what I say and do as I did if you have much of the volcano in you; but you will do better to listen, accept and adapt that which they tell you, *remembering* that this your apprenticeship as actor is but the very beginning of an exceedingly long apprenticeship as craftsman in all the crafts which go to make up the art.

When you have studied these thoroughly you will find some which are of value, and you will certainly find that the experience as actor has been necessary. The pioneer seldom finds an easy road, and as your way does not end in becoming a celebrated actor but is a much longer and an untrodden way leading to a very different end, you will have all the advantages and the disadvantages of pioneering; but keep in mind what I have told you: that your aim is *not* to become a celebrated actor, it is not to become the manager of a so-called successful theatre; it is not to become the producer of elaborate and much-talked-of plays; it is to become an artist of the Theatre; and as a base to all this you must, as I have said, serve your term of apprenticeship as actor faithfully and well. If at the end of five years as actor you are convinced that you know what your future will be; if, in fact, you are succeeding, you may give yourself up for lost. Short cuts lead nowhere in this world. Did you think when the longing came upon you and when you told your family that you must go upon the stage that such a great longing was to be so soon satisfied? Is satisfaction so small a thing? Is desire a thing of nothing, that a five years' quest can make a parody of it? But of course not. Your whole life is not too long, and then only at the very end will some small atom of what you have desired come to you. And so you will be still young when you are full of years.

ON THE ACTOR

As a man he ranks high, possesses generosity, and the truest sense of comradeship. I call to mind one actor whom I know and who shall stand as the type. A genial companion, and spreading a sense of companionship in the theatre; generous in giving assistance to younger and less accomplished actors, continually speaking about the work, picturesque in his manner, able to hold his own when standing at the side of the stage instead of in the centre; with a voice which commands my attention when I hear it, and, finally, with about as much knowledge of the art as a cuckoo has of anything which is at all constructive. Anything to be made according to plan or design is foreign to his nature. But his good nature tells him that others are on the stage besides himself, and that there must be a certain feeling of unity between their thoughts and his, yet this arrives by a kind of good-natured instinct and not through knowledge, and produces nothing positive. Instinct and experience have taught him a few things (I am not going to call them tricks), which he continually repeats. For instance, he has learned that the sudden drop in the voice from forte to piano has the power of accentuating and thrilling the audience as much as the crescendo from the piano into the forte. He also knows that laughter is capable of very many sounds, and not merely Ha, Ha, Ha. He knows that geniality is a rare thing on the stage and that the bubbling personality is always welcomed. But what he does not know is this, that this same bubbling personality and all this same instinctive knowledge doubles or even trebles its power when guided by scientific knowledge, that is to say, by art. If he should hear me say this now he would be lost in amazement and would consider that I was saying something which was finicking, dry, and not at all for the consideration of an artist. He is one who thinks that emotion creates emotion, and hates anything to do with calculation. It is not necessary for me to point out that all art has to do with calculation, and that the man who disregards this can only be but half an actor. Nature will not alone supply all which goes to create a work of art, for it is not the privilege of trees, mountains and brooks to create works of art, or everything which they touch would be given a definite and beautiful form. It is the particular power which belongs to man alone, and to him through his intelligence and his will. My friend probably thinks that Shakespeare wrote Othello in a passion of jealousy and that all he had to do was to write the first words which came into his mouth; but I am of the opinion, and I think others hold the same opinion, that the words had to pass through our author's head, and that it was just through this process and through the quality of his imagination and the strength of his brain that the richness of his nature was able to be entirely and clearly expressed, and by no other process could he have arrived at this.

Therefore it follows that the actor who wishes to perform Othello, let us say, must have not only the rich nature from which to draw his wealth, but must also have the imagination to know what to bring forth, and the brain to know how to put it before us. Therefore the ideal actor will be the man who possesses both a rich nature and a powerful brain. Of his nature we need not speak. It will contain everything. Of his brain we can say that the finer the brain the less liberty will it allow itself, remembering how much depends upon its co-worker, the Emotion, and also the less liberty will it allow its fellow-worker, knowing how valuable to it is its sternest control. Finally, the intellect would bring both itself and the emotions to so fine a sense of reason that the work would never boil to the bubbling point with its restless exhibition of activity, but would create that perfect moderate heat which it would know how to keep temperate. The perfect actor would be he whose brain could conceive and could show us the perfect symbols of all which his nature contains. He would not ramp and rage up and down in Othello, rolling his eyes and clenching his hands in order to give us an impression of jealousy; he would tell his brain to inquire into the depths, to learn all that lies there, and then to remove itself to another sphere, the sphere of the imagination, and there fashion certain symbols which, without exhibiting the bare passions, would none the less tell us clearly about them.

And the perfect actor who should do this would in time find out that the symbols are to be made mainly from material which lies outside his person. But I will speak to you fully about this when I get to the end of our talk. For then I shall show you that the actor as he is to-day must ultimately disappear and be merged in something else if works of art are to be seen in our kingdom of the Theatre.[1]

Meantime do not forget that the very nearest approach that has ever been to the ideal actor, with his brain commanding his nature, has been Henry Irving. There are many books which tell you about him, and the best of all the books is his face. Procure all the pictures, photographs, drawings, you can of him, and try to read what is there. To begin with you will find a mask, and the significance of this is most important. I think you will find it difficult to say when you look on the face, that it betrays the weaknesses which may have been in the nature. Try and conceive for yourself that face in movement—movement which was ever under the powerful control of the mind. Can you not see the mouth being made to move by the brain, and that same movement which is called expression creating a thought as definite as the line of a draughtsman does on a piece of paper or as a chord does in music? Cannot you see the slow turning of those eyes and the enlargement of them? These two movements alone contained so great a lesson for the future of the art of the theatre, pointed out so clearly the right use of expression as opposed to the wrong use, that it is amazing to me that many people have not seen more clearly what the future must be. I should say that the face of Irving was

[1] See *The Actor and the Über-Marionette,*" p. 54.

the connecting link between that spasmodic and ridiculous expression of the human face as used by the theatres of the last few centuries, and the masks which will be used in place of the human face in the near future.

Try and think of all this when losing hope that you will ever bring your nature as exhibited in your face and your person under sufficient command. Know for a truth that there is something other than your face and your person which you may use and which is easier to control. Know this, but make no attempt yet awhile to close with it. Continue to be an actor, continue to learn all that has to be learned, as to how they set about controlling the face, and then you will learn finally that it is not to be entirely controlled.

I give you this hope so that when this moment arrives you will not do as the other actors have done. They have been met by this difficulty and have shirked it, have compromised, and have not dared to arrive at the conclusion which an artist must arrive at if faithful to himself. That is to say, that the mask is the only right medium of portraying the expressions of the soul as shown through the expressions of the face.

ON THE STAGE-MANAGER

After you have been an actor you must become a stage-manager. Rather a misleading title this, for you will not be permitted to manage the stage. It is a peculiar position, and you can but benefit by the experience, though the experience will not bring either great delights to you or great results to the theatre in which you work. How well it sounds, this title, Stage-manager! it indicates "Master of the science of the stage."

Every theatre has a stage-manager, yet I fear there are no masters of the stage science. Perhaps already you are an under stage-manager. You will therefore remember the proud joy you felt when you were sent for, and, with some solemn words, informed that your manager had decided to advance you to the position of stage-manager, and begged to remind you of the importance of the post, and of the additional one or two pennies that go with the situation. I suppose that you thought that the great and last wonderful day of your dream had arrived, and you held your head a little higher for a week, and looked down on the vast land which seemed to stretch out before you.

But after then, what was it? Am I not right in saying that it meant an early attendance at the theatre to see after the carpenters, and whether the nails had been ordered, and whether the cards were fixed to the doors of the dressing-rooms? Am I not right in saying that you had to descend again to the stage and stand around waiting to see if things were done to time? whether the scenery was brought in and hung up to time? Did not the costumière come tearfully to you saying that some one had taken a dress from its box and substituted another? Did you not request the costumière to bring the offending party before you? and did you not have to manage these two in some tactful way so as to offend neither of them, and yet so as to get at the truth of the matter? And did you ever get at the truth of the matter? And did these two go away nursing anything but a loathèd hate towards you? Put the best case, one of them liked you, and the other began to intrigue against you the next hour. Did you find yourself still on the stage at about half-past ten, and did not the actors arrive at that hour apparently in total ignorance that you had been there already four hours, and with their superb conviction that the doors of the theatre had just that moment been opened because they had arrived? And did not at least six of these actors in the next quarter of an hour come up to you and with an "I say, old chap," or "Look here, old fellow," start asking you to arrange something for them on the stage so as to make their task a little easier? And were not the things which they asked all so opposed one to the other, that to assist any one actor would have been to offend the other five? Having told them that you would do your best, were you not relieved by the sudden appearance of the director of the theatre, generally the chief actor? And did you not instantly go to him with the different requests which had been made to you, hoping that he, as master, would take the responsibility of arranging all these difficult matters? And did he not reply to you, "Don't bother me with these details; please do what you think best," and did not you then instantly know in your heart that the whole thing was a farce—the title, the position, and all?

And then the rehearsal commenced. The first words are spoken; the first difficulty arrives. The play opens with a conversation between two gentlemen seated at a table. Having gone on for about five minutes, the director interrupts with a gentle question. He asks if he is not correct in saying that at yesterday's rehearsal Mr. Brown rose at this or that line, twisting his chair back with a sudden movement? The actor, a trifle distressed that he has been the cause of the first delay in the day's proceedings, and yet not wishing to take any fault to himself, asks with equal courtesy, "Are these the chairs which we are supposed to use on the night?" The director turns to the stage-manager, and asks him, "Are these the chairs we use upon the night?" "No, sir," replies the stage-manager. A momentary look of disapproval, ever so slight, passes from the director, and is reflected upon the faces of the two actors, and a little restless wind passes round the theatre. It is the first little hitch. "I think it would be best to use at rehearsal the chairs we are going to use on the night." "Certainly, sir!"

The stage-manager claps his hands. "Isherwood," he cries. A thin, sad-looking little man, with a mask which is impenetrable on account of its extreme sadness, comes on to the stage and stands before the judgment seat. He hesitates. "We shall use the chairs at rehearsal which have been ordered for this scene." "No chairs, sir, have been ordered for this scene." The wind rises. A sharp flash of lightning shows itself on the face of the director, and a sudden frown of thunder hangs upon the brows of the actors. The stage-manager asks to see the property list, that is to say, the list of things used in the scene. Isherwood casts his eyes pathetically across the desert of the stage in search of the leading lady. Being the wife of the director, she has seen no reason for arriving in time. When she arrives she will have the look upon her face of having been concerned with more important business elsewhere. Isherwood replies, "I had orders, sir, to put these two chairs in Scene II, as they are chairs with pink and red brocade." Great moment for the director. Thunder-clap. "Who gave you these orders?" "Miss Jones." [Miss Jones is the daughter of the leading lady, who is the wife of the director. Her position is not defined in the theatre, but she may be said to "assist her mother."] Hence the absence of the chairs. Hence the irritation of the entire company. Hence the waste of time in many theatres and certainly in many English theatres.

This is but one and the first trial of the stage-manager, who rather plays the part of the tyre than the axle of the wheel of the stage. The rehearsal continues. The stage-manager has to be there all the time with but little control and permitted to have less opinions, and yet held responsible for all errors; and after it is over, while the actors may retire to their luncheon, he must retire to the property room, the scene-painting room, the carpenters' room—must hear all their grievances, must see everything being delayed; and when the company returns to the theatre fresh after a pause of an hour or so he is expected to be as fresh and as good-humoured *without* a break of a minute. This would be an easy and pleasant matter if he had the authority of his title; that is to say, if in his contract lay the words "entire and absolute control of the stage and all that is on the stage."

But it is none the less a good if a strange experience. It teaches the man who assumes these terrible responsibilities how great a need there is for him to study the science of the stage, so that when it comes to his turn to be the director of the Theatre, he may dispense with the services of a so-called "stage-manager" by being the veritable stage-manager himself.

You will do well, after having remained an actor for five years to assume these difficult responsibilities of stage-manager for a year or two, and never forget that it is a position capable of development.

About the ideal stage-manager I have written in my book, *The Art of the Theatre*,[1] and I have shown there that the nature of his position should make him the most important figure in the whole world of the Theatre. It should therefore be your aim to become such a man, one who is able to take a play and produce it himself, rehearsing the actors and conveying to them the requirements of each movement, each situation; designing the scenery and the costumes and explaining to those who are to make them the requirements of these scenes and costumes; and working with the manipulators of the artificial light, and conveying to them clearly what is required.

Now, if I had nothing better to bring to you than these suggestions, if I had no further ideal, no further truth, to reveal to you about the Stage and about your future than this that I have told you of, I should consider that I had nothing to give you whatever and I should urge you to think no more of the Theatre. But I told you at the beginning of my letter that I was going to give you all sorts of things to cheer yourself with, so that you should have absolute faith in the greatness of the task which you set out to achieve; and here I remind you of this again lest you should think that this ideal manager of whom I speak is the ultimate

[1] This little book I have been able to rescue from a dungeon into which it had been thrown, and it is now free once more to roam the world under the protection of Mr. Heinemann. You will find it on p. 137 of this volume.

achievement possible for you. It is not. Read what I have written about him in *The Art of the Theatre*, and let that suffice you for the time being; but rest perfectly sure that I have more, much more to follow, and that your hope shall be so high, that no other hope, not even that of the poets or the priests, shall be higher.

To return to the duties of the stage-manager. I take it that I have already explained to you, or that you have already experienced, these ordinary difficulties, and that you have learned that great tact is required and no great talent. You have only to take care that in exercising this tact you do not become a little diplomatist, for a little diplomatist is a dangerous thing. Keep fresh your desire to emerge from that position, and your best way to do this is to study how to master the different materials which, later on, you will have to work in when your position is that of the ideal stage-manager. You will then possess your own Theatre, and what you place upon your stage will all be the work of your brain, much of it the work of your hands, and you must waste no time so as to be ready.

ON SCENE AND MOVEMENT

It is now time to tell you how I believe you may best become a designer of stage scenery and costumes, and how you may learn something about the uses of artificial light; how you may bring the actors who work with you to work in harmony with each other, with the scene, and, most of all, with the ideas of the author. You have been studying, and will go on studying, the works which you wish to present. Let us here limit them to the four great tragedies by Shakespeare. You will know these so well by the time you begin to prepare them for the stage, and the preparation will take you a year or two for each play; you will have no more doubts as to what impression you want to create; your exercise will be to see how best you can create that impression.

Let me tell you at the commencement that it is the large and sweeping impression produced by means of scene and the movement of the figures, which is undoubtedly the most valuable means at your disposal. I say this only after very many doubts and after much experience; and you must always bear in mind that it is from my experience that I speak, and that the best I can do is but to offer you that experience. Although you know that I haveparted company with the popular belief that the *written* play is of any deep and lasting value to the Art of the Theatre, we are not going so far as to dispense with it here. We are to accept it that the play still retains some value for us, and we are not going to waste that; our aim is to increase it. Therefore it is, as I say, the production of general and broad effects appealing to the eye which will add a value to that which has already been made valuable by the great poet.

First and foremost comes the *scene*. It is idle to talk about the distraction of scenery, because the question here is not how to create some distracting scenery, but rather how to create a place which harmonizes with the thoughts of the poet.

Come now, we take *Macbeth*. We know the play well. In what kind of place is that play laid? How does it look, first of all to our mind's eye, secondly to our eye?

I see two things. I see a lofty and steep rock, and I see the moist cloud which envelops the head of this rock. That is to say, a place for fierce and warlike men to inhabit, a place for phantoms to nest in. Ultimately this moisture will destroy the rock; ultimately these spirits will destroy the men. Now then, you are quick in your question as to what actually to create for the eye. I answer as swiftly—place there a rock! Let it mount up high. Swiftly I tell you, convey the idea of a mist which hugs the head of this rock. Now, have I departed at all for one eighth of an inch from the vision which I saw in the mind's eye?

But you ask me what form this rock shall take and what colour? What are the lines which are the lofty lines, and which are to be seen in any lofty cliff? Go to them, glance but a moment at them; now quickly set them down on your paper; *the lines and their direction*, never mind the cliff.

Do not be afraid to let them go high; they cannot go high enough; and remember that on a sheet of paper which is but two inches square you can make a line which seems to tower miles in the air, and you can do the same on your stage, for it is all a matter of proportion and nothing to do with actuality.

You ask about the colours? What are the colours that Shakespeare has indicated for us? Do not first look at Nature, but look in the play of the poet. Two; one for the rock, the man; one for the mist, the spirit. Now, quickly, take and accept this statement from me. Touch not a single other colour, but only these two colours through your whole progress of designing your scene and your costumes, yet forget not each that colour contains many variations. If you are timid for a moment and mistrust yourself or what I tell, when the scene is finished you will not see with your eye the effect you have seen with your mind's eye, when looking at the picture which Shakespeare has indicated.

It is this lack of courage, lack of faith in the value which lies in limitation and in proportion which is the undoing of all the good ideas which are born in the minds of the scene designers. They wish to make twenty statements at once. They wish to tell us not only of the lofty crag and the mist which clings to it; they wish to you tell of the moss of the Highlands and of the particular rain which descends in the month of August. They cannot resist showing that they know the form of the ferns of Scotland, and that their archæological research has been thorough in all matters relating to the castles of Glamis and Cawdor. And so in their attempt to tell us these many facts, they tell us nothing; all is confusion:

> "Most sacrilegious murder hath broke ope
> The Lord's anointed temple, and stole thence
> The life o' the building."

So, do as I tell you. Practise with the pencil on paper both on a small scale and on a large scale; practise with colour on canvas; so that you may see for yourself that what I say to you is true—and, if you are an Englishman, make haste: for if you do not others who read this in other countries will find in it technical truths and will outstrip you before you are aware of it. But the rock and its cloud of mist is not all that you have to consider. You have to consider that at the base of this rock swarm the clans of strange earthly forces, and that in the mist hover the spirits innumerable; to speak more technically, you have to think of the sixty or seventy actors whose movements have to be made at the base of the scene, and of the other figures which obviously may not be suspended on wires, and yet must be seen to be clearly separate from the human and more material beings.

It is obvious then that some curious sense of a dividing line must be created somewhere upon the stage so that the beholder, even if he look but with his corporal eye, shall be convinced that the two things are separate things. I will tell you how to do this. Line and proportion having suggested the material rock-like substance, tone and colour (one colour) will have given the ethereal to the mist-like vacuum. Now then, you bring this tone and colour downwards until it reaches nearly to the level of the floor; but you must be careful to bring this colour and this tone down in some place which is removed from the material rock-like substance.

You ask me to explain technically what I mean. Let your rock possess but half the width of the stage, let it be the side of a cliff round which many paths twist, and let these paths mingle in one flat space taking up half or perhaps three quarters of the stage. You have room enough there for all your men and women. Now then, open your stage and all other parts. Let there be a void below as well as above, and in this void let your mist fall and fade; and from that bring the figures which you have fashioned and which are to stand for the spirits. I know you are yet not quite comfortable in your mind about this rock and this mist; I know that you have got in the back of your head the recollection that a little later on in the play come several "interiors" as they are called. But, bless your heart, don't bother about that! Call to mind that the interior of a castle is made from the stuff which is taken from the quarries. Is it not precisely the same colour to begin with? and do not the blows of the axes which hew out the great stones give a texture to each stone which resembles the texture given it by natural means, as rain, lightning, frost? So you will not have to change your mind or change your impression as you proceed. You will have but to give variations of the same theme, the rock—the brown; the mist—the grey; and by these means you will, wonder of wonders, actually have preserved unity. Your success will depend upon your capacity to make variations upon these two themes; but remember never to let go of the main theme of the play when searching for variations in the scene.

By means of your scene you will be able to mould the movements of the actors, and you must be able to increase the impression of your numbers without actually adding another man to your forty or fifty. You must not, therefore, waste a single man, nor place him in such a position that an inch of him is lost. Therefore the place on which he walks must be the most carefully studied parts of the whole scene. But in telling you not to waste an inch of him I do not therefore mean to convey that you must *show* every inch of him. It is needless to say more on this point. By means of suggestion you may bring on the stage a sense of all things—the rain, the sun, the wind, the snow, the hail, the intense heat—but you will never bring them there by attempting to wrestle and close with Nature, in order so that you may seize some of her treasure and lay it before the eyes of the multitude. By means of suggestion in movement you may translate all the passions and the thoughts of vast numbers of people, or by means of the same you can assist your actor to convey the thoughts and the emotions of the particular character he impersonates. Actuality, accuracy of detail, is useless upon the stage.

Do you want further directions as to how to become a designer of scenes and how to make them beautiful, and, let us add for the sake of the cause, practical and inexpensive? I am afraid that if I were to commit my method to writing I should write something down which would prove not so much useless as bad. For it might be very dangerous for many people to imitate my method. It would be a different thing if you could study with me, practising what we speak about for a few years. Your nature would in time learn to reject that which was unsuited to it, and, by a daily and a much slower initiation, only the more important and valuable parts of my teaching would last. But I can give you now some more general ideas of things which you might do with advantage and things which you may leave undone. For instance, to begin with, don't worry—particularly don't worry your brain, and for Heaven's sake don't think it is important that you have got to do something, especially something clever.

I call to mind the amount of trouble I had when

I was a boy of twenty-one over the struggle to somehow produce designs traditional in character without feeling at all in sympathy with the tradition; and I count it as so much wasted time. I do not hold with others that it was of any value whatever. I remember making designs for scenes for *Henry IV*. I was working under an actor-manager at the time. I was working in a theatre where the chairs and the tables and other matters of detail played over-important and photographic parts, and, not knowing any better, I had to take all this as a good example. The play of *Henry IV*, therefore, consisted to my mind of one excellent part, Prince Hal, and thirty or forty other characters that trotted round this part. There was the usual table with the chairs round it on the right side. There at the back was the usual door, and I thought it rather unique and daring at the time to place this door a little bit off the straight. There was the window with the latches and the bolts and the curtains ruffled up to look as if they had been used for some time, and outside the glimpses of English landscape. There were the great flagons; and, of course, on the curtain rising there was to be a great cluster and fluster of "scurvy knaves," who ran in and out, and a noise of jovial drinkers in the next room. There was the little piece of jovial music to take up the curtain, that swinging jig tune which we have all grown so familiar with, there were the three girls who pass at the back of the window, laughing. One pops her head in at the window with a laugh and a word to the potman. Then there is the dwindling of the laughter and the sinking to piano of the orchestra as the first speaking character enters, and so on.

My whole work of that time was based on these stupid restless details which I had been led to suppose a production could be made from; and it was only when I banished the whole of this from my thoughts, and no longer permitted myself to see with the eyes of the producers of the period of Charles Kean, that I began to find anything fresh which might be of value to the play. And so for me to tell you how to make your scenes is well-nigh impossible. It would lead you into terrible blunders. I have seen some of the scenery which is supposed to be produced according to my teaching, and it is utter rubbish.

I let my scenes grow out of not merely the play, but from broad sweeps of thought which the play has conjured up in me, or even other plays by the same author have conjured up. For instance, the relation of *Hamlet* to *Macbeth* is quite close, and the one play may influence the other. I have been asked so many times, by people eager to make a little swift success or a little money, to explain to them carefully how I make my scenes; because, said they, with sweet simplicity, "then I could make some too." You will hardly believe it, but the strangest of people have said this to me, and if I could be of service to them without being treacherous to myself as an artist, and to the art, I would always do so. But you see how vain that would be! To tell them in five minutes or in five hours or even in a day how to do a thing which it has taken me a lifetime to begin to do would be utterly impossible. And yet when I have been unable to bring myself to tear my knowledge up into little shreds and give it to these people they have been most indignant, at times malignant.

And so you see it is not that I am unwilling to explain to you the size and shape of my back-cloths, the colour which is put upon them, the pieces of wood that are not to be attached to them, the way they are to be handled, the lights that are to be thrown upon them, and how and why I do everything else; it is only that if I were to tell you, though it might be of some service to you for the next two or three years, and you could produce several plays with enough "effects" therein to satisfy the curiosity of quite a number of people, though you would benefit to this extent you would lose to a far greater extent, and the art would have in me its most treacherous minister. We are not concerned with short cuts. We are not concerned with what is to be "*effective*" and what is to pay. We are concerned with the heart of this thing, and with loving and understanding it. Therefore approach it from all sides, surround it, and do not let yourself be attracted away by the idea of scene as an end in itself, of costume as an end in itself, or of stage management or any of these things, and never lose hold of your determination to win through to the secret—the secret which lies in the creation of another beauty, and then all will be well.

In preparing a play, while your mind is thinking of scene, let it instantly leap round and consider the acting, movement and voice. Decide nothing yet, instantly leap back to another thought about another part of this unit. Consider the movement robbed of all scene, all costume, merely as movement. Somehow mix the movement of the person with the movement which you see in your mind's eye in the scene. Now pour all your colour upon this. Now wash away all the colour. Now begin over again. Consider only the words. Wind them in and out of some vast and impossible picture, and now make that picture possible through the words. Do you see at all what I mean? Look at the thing from every standpoint and through every medium, and do not hasten to begin your work until one medium *force* you to commence. You can far sooner trust other influences to move your will and even your hand than you can trust your own little human brain. This may not be the methodical teachings of the school. The results they achieve are on record, and the record is nothing to boast about. Hard, matter-of-fact, mechanical teaching may be very good for a class, but it is not much good for the individual; and when I come to teach a class I shall not teach them so much by words as by practical demonstration.

By the way, I may tell you one or two things that you will find good not to do. For instance, do not trouble about the costume books. When in a great difficulty refer to one in order to see how little it will help you out of your difficulty, but your best plan is never to let yourself become complicated with these things. Remain clear and fresh. If you study how to draw a figure, how to put on it a jacket, coverings for the legs, covering for the head, and try to vary these coverings in all kinds of interesting, amusing, or beautiful ways, you will get much further than if you feast your eyes and confound your brain with Racinet, Planchet, Hottenroth and the others. The coloured costumes are the worst, and you must take great care with these and be utterly independent when you come to think about what you have been looking at. Doubt and mistrust them thoroughly. If you find afterwards that they contain many good things you will not be so far wrong; but if you accept them straight away your whole thought and sense for designing a costume will be lost; you will be able to design a Racinet costume or a Planchet costume, and you will lean far too much on these historically accurate men who are at the same time historically untrue.

Better than these that I have mentioned is Viollet le Duc. He has much love for the little

MUCH ADO ABOUT NOTHING

A Dancer.

"Charming costume, that," I hear some actor-manager say; "quite charming—so original, too—it's a pity it's impossible to make it. My wardrobe mistress tells me she couldn't make that because it's not clear."

This is typical of the withering praise such a design is met with when an anxious actor-manager catches sight of it. It is the habit *for some of them—one of them, I had almost written—to damn everything outside his own theatre as impossible, and in such a pathetic way, too. "You are not going to tell me that you* seriously *consider that is good," he asks of his visitor, and he adds, "I like mine much better"—"* mine *" is some little invention of one of his servants, for the great man never indulges himself that way.*

This costume design was carried out to perfection. One is obliged to state these things because of the story-tellers!

[Face page 32.

truths which underlie costume, and is very faithful in his attitude; but even his is more a book for the historical novelist, and one has yet to be written about imaginative costume. Keep continually designing such imaginative costumes. For example, make a barbaric costume; and a barbaric costume for a sly man which has nothing about it which can be said to be historical and yet is both sly and barbaric. Now make another design for another barbaric costume, for a man who is bold and tender. Now make a third for one who is ugly and vindictive. It will be an exercise. You will probably make blunders at first, for it is no easy thing to do, but I promise you if you persevere long enough you will be able to do it. Then go further; attempt to design the clothing for a divine figure and for a demonic figure: these of course will be studies in individual costumes, but the main strength of this branch of the work lies in the costume as mass. It is the mistake of all theatrical producers that they consider the costumes of the mass individually.

It is the same when they come to consider movements, the movements of masses on the stage. You must be careful not to follow the custom. We often hear it said that each member of the Meiningen Company composing the great crowd in *Julius Caesar* was acting a special part of his own. This may be very exciting as a curiosity, and attractive to a rather foolish audience, who would naturally say: "Oh, how interesting to go and look at one particular man in a corner who is acting a little part of his own! How wonderful! It is exactly like life!" And if that is the standard and if that is our aim, well and good.

But we know that it is not. Masses must be treated as masses, as Rembrandt treats a mass, as Bach and Beethoven treat a mass, and detail has nothing to do with the mass. Detail is very well in itself and in its place. You do not make an impression of mass by crowding a quantity of details together. Detail is made to form mass only by those people who love the elaborate, and it is a much easier thing to crowd a quantity of details together than it is to create a mass which shall possess beauty and interest. On the stage they instantly turn to the natural when they wish to create this elaborate structure. A hundred men to compose a crowd, or, let us say, all Rome, as in *Julius Caesar*; a hundred men, and each is told to act his little part. Each acts himself, giving vent to his own cries; each a different cry, though many of them copy the most effective ones, so that by the end of the first twenty nights they are all giving out the same cry. And each of them has his own action, which after the first twenty nights is exchanged for the most effective and popular action; and by this means a fairly decent crowd of men with waving arms and shouting voices may be composed, and may give some people the impression of a vast crowd. To others it gives the impression of a crush at a railway station.

Avoid all this sort of thing. Avoid the so-called "naturalistic" in movement as well as in scene and costume. The naturalistic stepped in on the Stage because the artificial had grown finicking, insipid; but do not forget that there is such a thing as *noble* artificiality.

Some one writing about natural movement and gesture says: "Wagner had long put in practice the system of *natural* stage action tried of late years at the Théâtre Libre in Paris by a French comedian; a system which, most happily, tends more and more to be generally adopted." It is to prevent such things being written that you exist.

This tendency towards the natural has nothing to do with art, and is abhorrent when it shows in art, even as artificiality is abhorrent when we meet it in everyday life. We must understand that the two things are divided, and we must keep each thing in its place; we cannot expect to rid ourselves in a moment of this tendency to be "natural"; to make "natural" scenes, and speak in a "natural" voice, but we can fight against it best by studying the other arts.

Therefore we have to put the idea of natural or unnatural action out of our heads altogether, and in place of it we have to consider *necessary or unnecessary action.* The necessary action at a certain moment may be said to be the natural action for that moment; and if that is what is meant by "natural," well and good. In so far as it is right it is natural, but we must not get into our heads that every haphazard natural action is right. In fact, there is hardly any action which is right, there is hardly any which is natural. Action is a way of spoiling something, says Rimbaud.

And to train a company of actors to show upon the stage the actions which are seen in every drawing-room, club, public-house or garret must seem to every one nothing less than tomfoolery. That companies are so trained is well known, but it remains almost incredible in its childishness. Just as I told you to invent costume which was significant, so must you invent a series of significant actions, still keeping in mind the great division which exists between action in the mass and action in the individual, and remembering that no action is better than little action.

I have told you to make designs for three costumes of a barbaric period, each particularized by some special character. Give action to these figures which you have made. Create for them significant actions, limiting yourself to those three texts that I have given you, the sly, the bold tenderness, the ugly and vindictive. Make studies for these, carry your little book or pieces of paper with you and continually be inventing with your pencil little hints of forms and faces stamped with these three impressions; and when you have collected dozens of them select the most beautiful.

And now for a word on this. I particularly did not say the most "effective," although I used the word "beautiful" as the artists use it, not as those of the stage use it.

I cannot be expected to explain to you all that the artist means by the word beautiful; but to him it is something which has the most balance about it, the *justest* thing, that which rings a complete and perfect bell note. Not the pretty, not the smooth, not the superb always, and not always the rich, seldom the "effective" as we know it in the Theatre, although at times that, too, is the beautiful. But Beauty is so vast a thing, and contains nearly all other things—contains even ugliness, which sometimes ceases to be what is held as ugliness, and contains harsh things, but never *incomplete* things.

Once let the meaning of this word *Beauty* begin to be thoroughly felt once more in the Theatre, and we may say that the awakening day of the Theatre is near. Once let the word *effective* be wiped off our lips, and they will be ready to speak this word Beauty. When we speak about the effective, we in the Theatre mean something which will reach across the foot lights. The old actor tells the young actor to raise his voice, to "Spit it out"—"Spit it out, laddie; fling it at the back of the gallery." Not bad advice either; but to think that this has not been learnt in the last five or six hundred years, and that we have not got *further*; that is what is so distressing about the whole business. Obviously all stage actions and all stage words must first of all be clearly seen, must be clearly heard. Naturally all pointed actions and all pointed speeches must have a clear and distinct form so that they may be clearly understood. We grant all this. It is the same in all art, and as with the other arts it goes without saying; but it is not the one and only essential thing which the elders must be continually drumming into the ears of the younger generation when it steps upon the stage. It teaches the young actor soon to become a master of tricks. He takes the short cut instinctively to these tricks, and this playing of tricks has been the cause of the invention of a word—"Theatrical," and I can put my finger on the reason why the young actor labours under this disadvantage the moment he begins his stage experience. It is because previous to his experience he has passed no time as student or as apprentice.

I do not know that I am such a great believer in the schools. I believe very much indeed in the general school which the world has to offer us, but there is this great difference between the "world" schooling of the actor and the "world" schooling of the other artists who do not go to the academies either. A young painter, or a young musician, a young poet, or a young architect, or a young sculptor may never enter an academy during his life, and may have ten years' knocking about in the world—learning here, learning there, experimenting and labouring unseen and his experiments unnoticed. The young actor may not enter an academy either, and he may also knock about in the world, and he too may experiment just the same as the others, but—and here is the vast difference—*all his experiments he must make in front of a public.* Every little atom of his work from the first day of his commencing until the last day of his apprenticeship must be seen, and must come under the fire of criticism. I shall ever be beholden to the higher criticism, and for a man of ten years' experience at any work to come under the fire of criticism will benefit him and his work a thousandfold. He has prepared himself; he has strength; he knows what he is going to face. But for every boy and girl to be subjected to this *the first year that they timidly attempt this enormous task is not only unfair on them but is disastrous to the art of the stage.*

Let us picture ourselves as totally new to this work. We are on fire with the desire to begin our work. Willingly and with an enormous courage we accept some small part. It is eight lines, and we appear for ten minutes. We are delighted, although almost in a panic. Say it is twenty lines. Do you think we say no? We are to appear six times, do you think we shall run away? We may not be angels, but we are certainly not fools for stepping in. It appears to us heaven. On we go. Next morning: "It is a pity that the manager elected an incompetent young man to fill so important a part."

I am not blaming the critic for writing this; I am not saying that it will kill a great artist or that it will break our heart; I only say that this seems so unfair that it is only natural that *we retaliate by taking an unfair advantage of the very art which we have commenced to love, by becoming* effective *at all costs.* We have received this criticism; we have done our best; the others have received good criticism; we can stand it no longer; we do as they do, we become *effective.* It takes most young actors but five years' acute suffering to become effective, to become theatrical. Too early criticism breaks the young actor who would be an artist as far as possible, and causes him to be a traitor to the art which he loves. Beware of this and rather be ineffective. Receive your bad criticism with a good grace and with the knowledge that with patience and with pride you can outlive and out-distance all around you. It is right that the critic should say that you were ineffective at a certain moment, or that you played your part badly, if you have been but three, four or five years on the stage, and if you are but still feeling your way slowly, instead of rushing to tricks for support. It is quite right of them to say that, for they are speaking the entire truth—you should be glad of this; but unconsciously they disclose a still greater truth. It is this—that the better the artist the worse the actor.

So take entire courage. Continue, as I have said at the beginning, to remain an actor until you can stand it no longer, until you feel you are on the point of giving way; then leap nimbly aside into the position of stage-manager. And here, as I have pointed out, you will be in a better position, if not a much better position, for are you approaching the point at which stands (slumbering, it is true) the muse of the theatre. Your most effective scenes, productions, costumes and the rest, will of course be the most theatrical ones. But here tradition is not so strong, and it is here that you will find something that you can rely on.

The critic is not more lenient towards the producer of plays, but somehow or other he is less inclined to use the word "effective." He seems to have a wider knowledge of the beauty or the ugliness of these things. It may be that the tradition of his art permits him this; for "production," as it is understood nowadays, is but a more modern development of the Theatre, and the critic has more liberty to say what he wishes. At any rate, when you become stage-manager, you will no longer have to appear each evening upon the stage in person, and therefore anything which is written about your work you cannot take as a personal criticism.

I thought to tell you here something about the uses of artificial light; but apply what I have said of scene and costume to this other branch as well. Some of it may apply. To tell you of the instruments which they use, how they use them so as to produce beautiful results, is not quite practical. If you have the wit to invent the scenes and the costumes that I have spoken about, you will soon have the wit to find your own way of using the artificial light we are given in the Theatre.

Finally, before we pass out of the Theatre on to other more serious matters, let me give you the last advice of all. When in doubt listen to the advice of a man in a theatre, even if he is only a dresser, rather than pay any attention to the amateur. A few painters, a few writers, and a few musicians, have used our Theatre as a kind of after-thought.

Take care to pay no attention to what they say or what they do. An ordinary stage hand knows more about our art than these amateurs. The painter has lately been making quite a pretty little raid upon the outskirts of the stage. He is very often a man of much intellectual ability and full of very many excellent theories, the old and beautiful theory of art which each in his own piece of soil knows how to cultivate best; and these theories he has exemplified in his own particular branch of art so well. In the Theatre they become sheer affectation. It is reasonable to suppose that a man who has spent fifteen to twenty years of his life painting in oils on a flat surface, etching on copper, or engraving on wood will produce something which is pictorial and has the qualities of the pictorial but nothing else. And so with the musician; he will produce something which is musical. So with the poet; he will produce something which is literary. It will all be very picturesque and pretty, but it will unfortunately be nothing to do with the Art of the Theatre. Beware of such men; you can do without them. If you have anything to do with them you will end by being an amateur yourself. If one of these should wish to talk with you about the Theatre be careful to ask him how long he has actually worked in a Theatre before you waste any more time listening to his unpractical theories.

And as the last but one word was about these men, so the last word of all shall be about their *work*. Their work is so fine, they have found such good laws and have followed these laws so well, have given up all their worldly hopes in this one great search after beauty, that when Nature seems to be too difficult to understand, go straight to these fellows, I mean to their work, and it will help you out of all the difficulties, for their works are the best and the wisest works in the world.

THE FUTURE. A HOPE

And now I intend to carry you on beyond this stage management about which I have spoken, and unveil to you some greater possibilities which I think are in store for you.

I have come to the end of talking with you about matters as they are, and I hope you will pass through those years as actor, manager, designer and producer without any very great disturbances. To do this successfully, although in your apprenticeship you must hold your own opinion, you must hold it very closely to yourself; and above all things remember that I do not expect you to hold my opinion or to stand up for it publicly. To do that would be to weaken your position and to weaken the value of this preparation time. It is of no value to me that people should be convinced of your belief in the truth of my statements, theories or practices: it is of great value to me that *you* should be so convinced. And so as to let nothing stand in the way of that I would have you run no risks, but keep our convictions to ourselves. Try to win no support for me. Run no risk of being faced with the dismissal from your post with the option of the denial of our mutual beliefs. Besides, there is no need for either of these two alternatives. I have taken so large a share of the rebuffs by loudly proclaiming my beliefs in the cause of the truth of this work, and am always prepared to take more if you will but leap forwards and secure the advantages, using me as the stalking-horse. I shall appreciate the fun, for there is a spice of fun in it all, and that will be my reward. Remember we are attacking a monster; a very powerful and subtle enemy; and when you signal to me let it be by that more secret means even than wireless telegraphy. I shall understand the communication.

When you have finished your apprenticeship, six to ten years, there will be no need to use further concealment: you will then be fitted to step out and, in your turn, unfurl your banner, for you will be upon the frontier of your kingdom, and about this kingdom I will speak now.

I use the word "Kingdom" instinctively in speaking of the land of the Theatre. It explains best what I mean. Maybe in the next three or four thousand years the word Kingdom will have disappeared—Kingdom, Kingship, King—but I doubt it; and if it does go something else equally fine will take its place. It will be the same thing in a different dress. You can't invent anything finer than Kingship, the idea of the King. It is merely another word for the Individual, the calm, shrewd personality; and so long as this world exists the calmest and the shrewdest personality will always be the King. In some rare instances he is called the President, but he is none the less the King. In some instances he is called the Pope, and sometimes the General; it all comes to the same thing, and it is no good denying it: He is the King. To the artist the thought is very dear. There is the sense of the perfect balancer. The king (to the artist) is that superb part of the scales, which the old workmen made in gold and sometimes touched with beautiful stones; the delicately worked handle without which the scales could not exist, and upon which the eye of the measurer must be fixed. Therefore I have taken as the device of our new art these scales, for our art is based upon the idea of perfect balance, the result of movement.

Here then is the thing which I promised at the beginning to bring to you. Having passed through your apprenticeship without having been merged in the trade, you are fitted to receive this. Without having done so you would not even be able to see it. I have no fear that what I throw to you now will be caught by other hands, because it is visible and tangible only to those who have passed through such an apprenticeship. In the beginning with you it was Impersonation; you passed on to Representation, and now you advance into Revelation. When impersonating and representing you made use of those materials which had always been made use of; that is to say, the human figure as exemplified in the actor, speech as exemplified in the poet through the actor, the visible world as shown by means of Scene. You now will reveal by means of movement the invisible things, those seen through the eye and not with the eye, by the wonderful and divine power of Movement.

There is a thing which man has not yet learned to master, a thing which man dreamed not was waiting for him to approach with love; it was invisible and yet ever present with him. Superb in its attraction and swift to retreat, a thing waiting.

but for the approach of the right men, prepared to soar with them through all the circles beyond the earth—it is Movement.

It is somehow a common belief that only by means of words can truths be revealed. Even the wisdom of China has said: "Spiritual truth is deep and wide, of infinite excellence, but difficult of comprehension. Without words it would be impossible to expound its doctrine; without images its form could not be revealed. Words explain the law of two and six, images delineate the relation of four and eight. Is it not profound, as infinite as space, beyond all comparison lovely?"

But what of that infinite and beautiful thing dwelling in space called Movement? From sound has been drawn that wonder of wonders called Music. Music, one could speak of it as St. Paul speaks of love. It is all love, it is all that he says true love should be. It suffereth all things, and is kind; is not puffed up, doth not behave itself unseemly; believeth all things, hopeth all things—how infinitely noble.

And as like one sphere to another, so is Movement like to Music. I like to remember that all things spring from movement, even music; and I like to think that it is to be our supreme honour to be the ministers to the supreme force—movement. For you see where the theatre (even the poor distracted and desolate theatre) is connected with this service. The theatres of all lands, east and west, have developed (if a degenerate development) from movement, the movement of the human form. We know so much, for it is on record : and before the human being assumed the grave responsibility of using his own person as an instrument through which this beauty should pass, there was another and a wiser race, who used other instruments.

In the earliest days the dancer was a priest or a priestess, and not a gloomy one by any means; too soon to degenerate into something more like the acrobat, and finally to achieve the distinction of the ballet-dancer. By association with the minstrel, the actor appeared. I do not hold, that with the renaissance of the dance comes the renaissance of the ancient art of the Theatre, for I do not hold that the ideal dancer is the perfect instrument for the expression of all that is most perfect in movement. The ideal dancer, male or female, is able by the strength or grace of the body to express much of the strength and grace which is in human nature, but it cannot express all, nor a thousandth part of that all. For the same truth applies to the dancer and to all those who use their own person as instrument. Alas! the human body refuses to be an instrument, even to the mind which lodges in that body. The sons of Los rebelled and still rebel against their father. The old divine unity, the divine square, the peerless circle of our nature has been ruthlessly broken by our moods, and no longer can instinct design the square or draw the circle on the grey wall

JULIUS CAESAR

ACT II. SCENE II.

Before you like or dislike this design will you do me the fairness of reading Act II. scene ii. It's an exciting scene, and will repay your pains.

Then, if you are an actor-manager and you dislike it, will you design a better? If only one of these so-called actor-manager-producers, who never have really "produced" anything, would let us all see him designing anything, I'm sure we should all be more than willing to applaud his honest endeavours and perhaps his achievement. As it is, he has to call in people to do his work for him. Hence the awful expense—hence the patchwork results—the dishonesty of the whole system.

[illegible]

Act II, Scene II.

Before you like or dislike this design [illegible] of making Act II, Scene [illegible] your [illegible]

Then, if you are [illegible] will design a better? If only one of [illegible] producers, who never have really "produced" anything, would let us all see [illegible] anything [illegible] more than adding to [illegible] his achievement. [illegible] work for him. [illegible] results—the dishonesty of the whole system.

[Face page 48.

before it. But with a significant gesture we thrill our souls once more to advance without our bodies upon a new road and win it all back again. This is a truth which is not open to argument, and a truth which does not lessen the beauty which exhales from the dearest singer or the dearest dancer of all times.

To me there is ever something more seemly in man when he invents an instrument which is outside his person, and through that instrument translates his message. I have a greater admiration for the organ, for the flute and for the lute than I have for the human voice when used as instrument. I have a greater feeling of admiration and fitness when I see a machine which is made to fly than when I see a man attaching to himself the wings of a bird. For a man through his person can conquer but little things, but through his mind he can conceive and invent that which shall conquer all things.

I believe not at all in the personal magic of man, but only in his impersonal magic. It seems to me that we should not forget that we belong to a period after the Fall and not before it. I can at least extract a certain hint from the old story. And though it may be only a story, I feel that it is just the very story for the artist. In that great period previous to this event we can see in our mind's eye the person of man in so perfect a state that merely to wish to fly was to fly, merely to desire that which we call the impossible was to achieve it. We seem to see man flying into the air or diving into the depths and taking no harm therefrom. We see no foolish clothes, we are aware of no hunger and thirst. But now that we are conscious that this "square deific" has been broken in upon, we must realize that no longer is man to advance and proclaim that his person is the perfect and fitting medium for the expression of the perfect thought.

So we have to banish from our mind all thought of the use of a human form as the instrument which we are to use to translate what we call *Movement*. We shall be all the stronger without it. We shall no longer waste time and courage in a vain hope. The exact name by which this art will be known cannot yet be decided on, but it would be a mistake to return and look for names in China, India or Greece. We have words enough in our English language, and let the English word become familiar to the tongues of all the nations. I have written elsewhere, and shall continue to write, all about this matter as it grows in me, and you from time to time will read what I write. But I shall not remove from you the very difficulty which will be the source of your pleasure; I wish to leave all open and to make no definite rules as to how and by what means these movements are to be shown. This alone let me tell you. I have thought of and begun to make my instrument, and through this instrument I intend soon to venture in my quest of beauty. How do I know whether I can achieve that or not?

Therefore how can I tell you definitely what are the first rules which you have to learn ? Alone and unaided I can reach no final results. It will need the force of the whole race to discover all the beauties which are in this great source, this new race of artists to which you belong. When I have constructed my instrument, and permitted it to make its first assay, I look to others to make like instruments. Slowly, and from the principles which rule all these instruments some better instrument will be made.

I am guided in the making of mine by only the very first and simplest thoughts which I am able to see in movement. The subtleties and the complicated beauties contained in movement as it is seen in Nature, these I dare not consider; I do not think I shall ever be able to hope to approach these. Yet that does not discourage me from attempting some of the plainest, barest and simplest movements; I mean those which seem to me the simplest, those which I seem to understand. And after I have given activity to those I suppose I shall be permitted to continue to give activity to the like of them; but I am entirely conscious that they contain but the simplest of rhythms, the great movements will not yet be captured, no, not for thousands of years. But when they come, great health comes with them, for we shall be nearer balance than we have ever been before.

I think that movement can be divided into two

distinct parts, the movement of two and four which is the square, the movement of one and three which is the circle. There is ever that which is masculine in the square and ever that which is feminine in the circle And it seems to me that before the female spirit gives herself up, and with the male goes in quest of this vast treasure, perfect movement will not be discovered; at least, I like to suppose all this.

And I like to suppose that this art which shall spring from movement will be the first and final belief of the world; and I like to dream that for the first time in the world men and women will achieve this thing together. How fresh, how beautiful it would be! And as this is a new beginning it lies before men and before women of the next centuries as a vast possibility. In men and women there is a far greater sense of movement than of music. Can it be that this idea which comes to me now will at some future date blossom through help of the woman?—or will it be, as ever, the man's part to master these things alone? The musician is a male, the builder is a male, the painter is a male, and the poet is a male.

Come now, here is an opportunity to change all this. But I cannot follow the thoughts any farther here, neither will you be able to.

Get on with the thought of the invention of an instrument by which means you can bring movement before our eyes. When you have reached this point in your developments you need have no further fear of hiding your feeling or your opinion, but may step forward and join me in the search. You will not be a revolutionary against the Theatre, for you will have risen above the Theatre, and entered into something beyond it. Maybe you will pursue a scientific method on your search, and that will lead to very valuable results. There must be a hundred roads leading to this point—not merely one; and a scientific demonstration of all that you may discover can in no way harm this thing.

Well, do you see any value in the thing I give you ? If you do not at first you will by and by. I could not expect a hundred or even fifty, no, not ten, to understand. But *one ?* It is possible —just possible. And *that* one will understand that I write here of things, dealing with to-day—dealing with to-morrow and with the future, and he will be careful not to confound these three separate periods.

I believe in each period and in the necessity of undergoing the experience each has to offer.

I believe in the time when we shall be able to create works of art in the Theatre without the use of the written play, without the use of actors; *but* I believe also in the necessity of daily work under the conditions which are to-day offered us.

The word TO-DAY is good, and the word TO-MORROW is good, and the words THE FUTURE are divine—but the word which links all these words is more perfect than all; it is that balancing word AND.

THE ACTOR AND THE ÜBER-MARIONETTE

INSCRIBED IN ALL AFFECTION TO MY GOOD FRIENDS, DE VOS AND ALEXANDER HEVESI

"TO SAVE THE THEATRE, THE THEATRE MUST BE DESTROYED, THE ACTORS AND ACTRESSES MUST ALL DIE OF THE PLAGUE. . . . THEY MAKE ART IMPOSSIBLE."—ELEONORA DUSE: *Studies in Seven Arts*, ARTHUR SYMONS. (CONSTABLE, 1900.)

IT has always been a matter for argument whether or no Acting is an art, and therefore whether the actor is an Artist, or something quite different. There is little to show us that this question disturbed the minds of the leaders of thought at any period, though there is much evidence to prove that had they chosen to approach this subject as one for their serious consideration, they would have applied to it the same method of inquiry as used when considering the arts of Music and Poetry, of Architecture, Sculpture and Painting.

On the other hand there have been many warm arguments in certain circles on this topic. Those taking part in it have seldom been actors, very rarely men of the Theatre at all, and all have displayed any amount of illogical heat and very little knowledge of the subject. The arguments against acting being an art, and against the actor being an artist, are generally so unreasonable and so personal in their detestation of the actor, that I think it is for this reason the actors have taken no trouble to go into the matter. So now regularly with each season comes the quarterly attack on the actor and on his jolly calling; the attack usually ending in the retirement of the enemy. As a rule it is the literary or private gentlemen who fill the enemy's rank. On the strength of having gone to see plays all their lives, or on the strength of never having gone to see a play in their lives, they attack for some reason best known to themselves. I have followed these regular attacks season by season, and they seem mostly to spring from irritability, personal enmity, or conceit. They are illogical from beginning to end. There can be no such attack made on the actor or his calling. My intention here is not to join in any such attempt; I would merely place before you what seem to me to be the logical facts of a curious case, and I believe that these admit of no dispute whatever.

ACTING is not an art. It is therefore incorrect to speak of the actor as an artist. For accident is an enemy of the artist. Art is the exact antithesis of pandemonium, and pandemonium is created by the tumbling together of many accidents. Art arrives only by design. Therefore in order to make any work of art it is clear we may only work in those materials with which we can calculate. Man is not one of these materials.

The whole nature of man tends towards freedom; he therefore carries the proof in his own person that as *material* for the Theatre he is useless. In the modern theatre, owing to the use of the bodies of men and women *as their material*, all which is presented there is of an accidental nature. The actions of the actor's body, the expression of his face, the sounds of his voice, all are at the mercy of the winds of his emotions: these winds, which must blow for ever round the artist, moving without unbalancing him. But with the actor, emotion *possesses* him; it seizes upon his limbs, moving them whither it will. He is at its beck and call, he moves as one in a frantic dream or as one distraught, swaying here and there; his head, his arms, his feet, if not utterly beyond control, are so weak to stand against the torrent of his passions, that they are ready to play him false at any moment. It is useless for him to attempt to reason with himself. Hamlet's calm directions (the dreamer's, not the logician's directions, by the way) are thrown to the winds. His limbs refuse, and refuse again to obey his mind the instant emotion warms, while the mind is all the time creating the heat which shall set these emotions afire. As with his movement, so is it with the expression of his face. The mind struggling and succeeding for a moment, in moving the eyes, or the muscles of the face whither it will; the mind bringing the face for a few moments into thorough subjection, is suddenly swept aside by the emotion which has grown hot through the action of the mind. Instantly, like lightning, and before the mind has time to cry out and protest, the hot passion has mastered the actor's expression. It shifts and changes, sways and turns, it is chased by emotion from the actor's forehead between his eyes and down to his mouth; now he is entirely at the mercy of emotion, and crying out to it: "Do with me what you will!" His expression runs a mad riot hither and thither, and lo! "Nothing is coming of nothing." It is the same with his voice as it is with his movements. Emotion cracks the voice of the actor. It sways his voice to join in the conspiracy against his mind. Emotion works upon the voice of the actor, and he produces the impression of discordant emotion. It is of no avail to say that emotion is the spirit of the gods, and is precisely what the artist aims to produce; first of all this is not true, and even if it were quite true, every stray emotion, every casual feeling, cannot be of value. Therefore the mind of the actor, we see, is less powerful than his emotion, for emotion is able to win over the mind to assist in the destruction of that which the mind would produce; and as the mind becomes the slave of the emotion it follows that accident upon accident must be continually occurring. So then, we have arrived at this point: that emotion is the cause which first of all creates, and secondly destroys. Art, as we have said, can admit of no accidents. That, then, which the actor gives us, is not a work of art; it is a series of accidental confessions. In the beginning the human body was not used as material in the Art of the Theatre. In the beginning the emotions of men and women were not considered as a fit exhibition for the multitude. An elephant and a tiger in an arena suited the taste better, when the desire was to excite. The passionate tussle between the elephant and the tiger gives us all the excitement that we can get from the modern stage, and can give it us unalloyed. Such an exhibition is not more brutal, it is more delicate, it is more humane; for there is nothing more outrageous than that men and women should be let loose on a platform, so that they may expose that which artists refuse to show except veiled, in the form which their minds create. How it was that man was ever persuaded to take the place which until that time animals had held is not difficult to surmise.

The man with the greater learning comes across the man with the greater temperament. He addresses him in something like the following terms: "You have a most superb countenance; what magnificent movements you make! Your voice, it is like the singing of birds; and how your eye flashes! What a noble impression you give!

You almost resemble a god! I think all people should have pointed out to them this wonder which is contained in you. I will write a few words which you shall address to the people. You shall stand before them, and you shall speak my lines just as you will. It is sure to be perfectly right."

And the man of temperament replies: "Is that really so? Do I strike you as appearing as a god? It is the very first time I have ever thought of it. And do you think that by appearing in front of the people I could make an impression which might benefit them, and would fill them with enthusiasm? "No, no, no," says the intelligent man; "by no means only by *appearing;* but if you have something to say you will indeed create a great impression."

The other answers: "I think I shall have some difficulty in speaking your lines. I could easier just appear, and say something instinctive, such as 'Salutation to all men!' I feel perhaps that I should be able to be more myself if I acted in that way." "That is an excellent idea," replies the tempter, "that idea of yours: 'Salutation to all men!' On that theme I will compose say one hundred or two hundred lines; you'll be the very man to speak those lines. You have yourself suggested it to me. Salutation! Is it agreed, then, that you will do this?" "If you wish it," replies the other, with a good-natured lack of reason, and flattered beyond measure.

And so the comedy of author and actor commences. The young man appears before the multitude and speaks the lines, and the speaking of them is a superb advertisement for the art of literature. After the applause the young man is swiftly forgotten; they even forgive the way he has spoken the lines; but as it was an original and new idea at the time, the author found it profitable, and shortly afterwards other authors found it an excellent thing to use handsome and buoyant men *as instruments*. It mattered nothing to them that the instrument was a human creature. Although they knew not the stops of the instrument, they could play rudely upon him and they found him useful. And so to-day we have the strange picture of a man content to give forth the thoughts of another, which that other has given form to while at the same time he exhibits his person to the public view. He does it because he is flattered; and vanity—will not reason. But all the time, and however long the world may last, the nature in man will fight for freedom, and will revolt against being made a slave or medium for the expression of another's thoughts. The whole thing is a very grave matter indeed, and it is no good to push it aside and protest that the actor is not the medium for another's thoughts, and that he invests with life the dead words of an author; because even if this were true (true it cannot be), and even if the actor were to present none but the ideas which he himself should compose, his nature would still be in servitude; his body would have to become the slave of his mind; and that, as I have shown, is what the healthy body utterly refuses to do. Therefore the body of man, for the reason which I have given, is *by nature* utterly useless as a material for an art. I am fully aware of the sweeping character of this statement; and as it concerns men and women who are alive, and who as a class are ever to be loved, more must be said lest I give unintentional offence. I know perfectly well that what I have said here is not yet going to create an exodus of all the actors from all the theatres in the world, driving them into sad monasteries where they will laugh out the rest of their lives, with the Art of the Theatre as the main topic for amusing conversation. As I have written elsewhere, the Theatre will continue its growth and actors will continue for some years to hinder its development. But I see a loop-hole by which in time the actors can escape from the bondage they are in. They must create for themselves a new form of acting, consisting for the main part of symbolical gesture. To-day they *impersonate* and interpret; to-morrow they must *represent* and interpret; and the third day they must create. By this means style may return. To-day the actor impersonates a certain being. He cries to the audience: "Watch me; I am now pretending to be so and so, and I am now pretending to do so and so;" and then he proceeds to *imitate* as exactly as possible, that which he has announced he will *indicate*. For instance, he is Romeo. He tells the audience that he is in love, and he proceeds to show it, by kissing Juliet. This, it is claimed, is a work of art: it is claimed for this that it is an intelligent way of suggesting thought. Why—why, that is just as if a painter were to draw upon the wall a picture of an animal with long ears and then write under it "This is a donkey." The long ears made it plain enough, one would think, without the inscription, and any child of ten does as much. The difference between the child of ten and the artist is that the artist is he who by drawing certain signs and shapes creates the impression of a donkey: and the greater artist is he who creates the impression of the whole genus of donkey, the *spirit* of the thing.

The actor looks upon life as a photo-machine looks upon life; and he attempts to make a picture to rival a photograph. He never dreams of his art as being an art such for instance as music. He tries to reproduce Nature; he seldom thinks to invent with the aid of Nature, and he never dreams of *creating*. As I have said, the best he can do when he wants to catch and convey the poetry of a kiss, the heat of a fight, or the calm of death, is to copy slavishly, photographically—he kisses—he fights—he lies back and mimics death—and, when you think of it, is not all this dreadfully stupid? Is it not a poor art and a poor cleverness, which cannot convey the spirit and essence of an idea to an audience, but can only show an artless copy, a facsimile of the thing itself? This is to be an imitator, not an artist. This is to claim kinship with the ventriloquist.[1]

There is a stage expression of the actor "getting under the skin of the part." A better one would be getting "*out* of the skin of the part altogether." "What, then," cries the red-blooded and flashing actor, "is there to be no flesh and blood in this same art of the theatre of yours? No life?" It depends what you call life, signor, when you use the word in relation with the idea of art. The painter means something rather different to actuality when he speaks of life in his art, and the other artists generally mean something essentially spiritual; it is only the actor, the ventriloquist, or the animal-stuffer who, when they speak of putting life into their work, mean some actual and lifelike

[1] "And therefore when any one of these pantomimic gentlemen, who are so clever that they can imitate anything, comes to us, and makes a proposal to exhibit himself and his poetry, we will fall down and worship him as a sweet and holy and wonderful being; but we must also inform him that in our State such as he are not permitted to exist: the law will not allow them. And so, when we have anointed him with myrrh, and set a garland of wool upon his head, we shall lead him away to another city. For we mean to employ for our soul's health the rougher and severer poet or story-teller, who will imitate the style of the virtuous only, and will follow those models which we prescribed at first when we began the education of our soldiers."—PLATO. [The whole passage being too long to print here, we refer the reader to *The Republic*, Book III. p. 395.]

reproduction, something blatant in its appeal, that it is for this reason I say that it would be better if the actor should get out of the skin of the part altogether. If there is any actor who is reading this, is there not some way by which I can make him realize the preposterous absurdity of this delusion of his, this belief that he should aim to make an actual copy, a reproduction ? I am going to suppose that such an actor is here with me as I talk; and I invite a musician and a painter to join us. Let them speak. I have had enough of seeming to decry the work of the actor from trivial motives. I have spoken this way because of my love of the Theatre, and because of my hopes and belief that before long an extraordinary development is to raise and revive that which is failing in the Theatre, and my hope and belief that the actor will bring the force of his courage to assist in this revival. My attitude towards the whole matter is misunderstood by many in the Theatre. It is considered to be *my* attitude, mine alone; a stray quarreller I seem to be in their eyes, a pessimist, grumbling; one who is tired of a thing and who attempts to break it. Therefore let the other artists speak with the actor, and let the actor support his own case as best he may, and let him listen to their opinion on matters of art. We sit here conversing, the actor, the musician, the painter and myself. I who represent an art distinct from all these, shall remain silent.

As we sit here, the talk first turns upon Nature. We are surrounded by beautiful curving hills and trees, vast and towering mountains in the distance covered with snow; around us innumerable delicate sounds of Nature stirring—Life. "How beautiful," says the painter, "how beautiful the sense of all this!" He is dreaming of the almost impossibility of conveying on to his canvas the full earthly and spiritual value of that which is around him, yet he faces the thing as man generally faces that which is most dangerous. The musician gazes upon the ground. The actor's is an inward and personal gaze at himself. He is unconsciously enjoying the sense of himself, as representing the main and central figure in a really good scene. He strides across the space between us and the view, sweeping in a half circle, and he regards the superb panorama without seeing it, conscious of one thing only, himself and his attitude. Of course an actress would stand there meek in the presence of Nature. She is but a little thing, a little picturesque atom; for picturesque we know she is in every movement, in the sigh which, almost unheard by the rest of us, she conveys to her audience and to herself, that she is there, "little me," in the presence of the God that made her, and all the rest of the sentimental nonsense. So we are all collected here, and having taken the attitudes natural to us, we proceed to question each other. And let us imagine that for once we are all really interested in finding out all about the other's interests, and the other's work. (I grant that this is very unusual, and that mind-selfishness, the highest form of stupidity, encloses many a professed artist somewhat tightly in a little square box.) But let us take it for granted that there is a general interest; that the actor and the musician wish to learn something about the art of painting; and that the painter and the musician wish to understand from the actor what his work consists of and whether and why he considers it an art. For here they shall not mince matters, but shall speak that which they believe. As they are looking only for the truth, they have nothing to fear; they are all good fellows, all good friends; not thin-skinned, and can give and take blows. "Tell us," asks the painter, "is it true that before you can act a part properly you must feel the emotions of the character you are representing?" "Oh well, yes and no; it depends what you mean," answers the actor. "We have first to be able to feel and sympathize and also criticize the emotions of a character; we look at it from a distance before we close with it: we gather as much as we can from the text and we call to mind all the emotions suitable for this character to exhibit. After having many times rearranged and selected those emotions which we consider of importance we then practise to reproduce them before the audience; and in order to do so we must feel as little as is necessary; in fact the less we feel, the firmer will our hold be upon our facial and bodily expression." With a gesture of genial impatience, the artist rises to his feet and paces to and fro. He had expected his friend to say that it had nothing whatever to do with emotions, and that he could control his face, features, voice and all, just as if his body were an instrument. The musician sinks down deeper into his chair. "But has there never been an actor," asks the artist, "who has so trained his body from head to foot that it would answer to the workings of his mind without permitting the emotions even so much as to awaken? Surely there must have been one actor, say one out of ten millions, who has done this?." "No," says the actor emphatically, "never, never; there never has been an actor who reached such a state of mechanical perfection that his body was *absolutely* the slave of his mind. Edmund Kean of England, Salvini of Italy, Rachel, Eleonora Duse, I call them all to mind and I repeat there never was an actor or actress such as you describe." The artist here asks: "Then you admit that it would be a state of perfection?" "Why, of course! But it is impossible; will always be impossible," cries the actor; and he rises—almost with a sense of relief. "That is as much as to say, there never was a perfect actor, there has never been an actor who has not spoiled his performance once, twice, ten times, sometimes a hundred times, during the evening? There never has been a piece of acting which could be called even almost perfect, and there never will be ?" For answer the actor asks quickly: "But has there been ever a painting, or a piece of architecture, or a piece of music which may be called perfect ?" "Undoubtedly," they reply. "The laws which control our arts make such a thing possible." "A picture, for instance," continues the artist, "may consist of four lines, or four hundred lines, placed in certain positions; it may be as simple as possible, but it is possible to make it perfect. That is to say, I can first choose that which is to make the lines; I can choose that on which I am to place the lines: I can consider this as long as I like; I can alter it; then in a state which is both free from excitement, haste, trouble, nervousness—in fact, in any state I choose (and of course I prepare, wait, and select that also)—I can put these lines together—so—now they are in their place. Having my material, nothing except my own will can move or alter these; and, as I have said, my own will is entirely under my control. The line can be straight or it can wave; it can be round if I choose, and there is no fear that when I wish to make a straight line I shall make a curved one, or that when I wish to make a curved there will be square parts about it. And when it is ready—finished—it undergoes no change but that which Time, who finally destroys it, wills." "That is rather an extraordinary thing," replies the actor; "I wish it were possible in my work." "Yes," replies the artist, "*it is a very extraordinary thing*, and it is that which I hold makes the difference between an intelligent statement and a casual or haphazard statement. The most intelligent statement, that is a work of art. The haphazard statement, that is a work of chance. When the intelligent statement reaches its highest possible form it becomes a work of fine art. And therefore I have always held, though I may be mistaken, that your work has not the nature of an art. That is to say (and you have said it yourself) each statement that you make in your work is subject to every conceivable change which emotion chooses to bring about. That which you conceive in your mind, your body is not permitted by Nature to complete. In fact, your body, gaining the better of your intelligence, has in many instances on the stage driven out the intelligence altogether. Some actors seem to say: 'What value lies in having beautiful ideas? To what end shall my mind conceive a fine idea, a fine thought, for my body, which is so entirely beyond my control, to spoil? I will throw my mind overboard, let my body pull me and the play through;' and there seems to me to be some wisdom in the standpoint of such an actor. He does not dilly-dally between the two things which are contending in him, the one against the other. He is not a bit afraid of the result. He goes at it like a man, sometimes a trifle too like a centaur;

he flings away all science, all caution, all reason, and the result is good spirits in the audience, and for that they pay willingly. But we are here talking about other things than excellent spirits, and though we applaud the actor who exhibits such a personality as this, I feel that we must not forget that we are applauding his personality, *he* it is we applaud, not what he is doing or how he is doing it; nothing to do with art at all, absolutely nothing to do with art, with calculation, or design." "You're a nice friendly creature," laughs the actor gaily, "telling me my art's no art! But I believe I see what you mean. You mean to say that before I appear on the stage, and before my body commences to come into the question, I am an artist." "Well, yes, *you* are, you happen to be, because you are a very bad actor; you're abominable on the stage, but you have ideas, you have imagination; you are rather an exception, I should say. I have heard you tell me how you would play Richard III; what you would do; what strange atmosphere you would spread over the whole thing; and that which you have told me you have seen in the play, and that which you have invented and added to it, is so remarkable, so consecutive in its thought, so distinct and clear in form, that *if* you could make your body into a machine, or into a dead piece of material such as clay; and *if* it could obey you in every movement for the entire space of time it was before the audience; and *if* you could put aside Shakespeare's poem—you would be able to make a work of art out of that which is in you. For you would not only have dreamt, you would have executed to perfection; and that which you had executed could be repeated time after time without so much difference as between two farthings." "Ah," sighs the actor, "you place a terrible picture before me. You would prove to me that it is impossible for us ever to think of ourselves as artists. You take away our finest dream, and you give us nothing in its place." "No, no, that's not for me to give you. That's for you to find. Surely there must be laws at the roots of the Art of the Theatre, just as there are laws at the roots of all true arts, which if found and mastered would bring you all you desire?" "Yes, the search would bring the actors to a wall." "Leap it, then!" "Too high!" "Scale it, then!" "How do we know where it would lead?" "Why, up and over." "Yes, but that's talking wildly, talking in the air." "Well, that's the direction you fellows have to go; fly in the air, live in the air. Something will follow when some of you begin to. I suppose," continues he, "you will get at the root of the matter in time, and then what a splendid future opens before you! In fact, I envy you. I am not sure I do not wish that photography had been discovered before painting, so that we of this generation might have had the intense joy of advancing, showing that photography was pretty well in its way, but there was something better!" "Do you hold that our work is on a level with photography?" "No, indeed, it is not half as exact. It is less of an art even than photography. In fact, you and I, who have been talking all this time while the musician has sat silent, sinking deeper and deeper into his chair, our arts by the side of his art, are jokes, games, absurdities." At which the musician must go and spoil the whole thing by getting up and giving vent to some foolish remark. The actor immediately cries out, "But I don't see that that's such a wonderful remark for a representative of the only art in the world to make," at which they all laugh—the musician in a sort of crest-fallen, conscious manner. "My dear fellow, that is just because he is a musician. He is nothing except in his music. He is, in fact, somewhat unintelligent, except when he speaks in notes, in tones, and in the rest of it. He hardly knows our language, he hardly knows our world, and the greater the musician, the more is this noticeable; indeed it is rather a bad sign when you meet a composer who is intelligent. And as for the intellectual musician, why, that means another——; but we mustn't whisper that name here—he is so popular to-day. What an actor the man would have been, and what a personality he had! I understand that all his life he had yearnings towards being an actor, and

I believe he would have been an excellent comedian, whereas he became a musician—or was it a playwright? Anyhow, it all turned out a great success—a success of personality." "Was it not a success of art?" asks the musician. "Well, which art do you mean?" "Oh, all the arts combined," he replies, blunderingly but placidly. "How can that be? How can all arts combine and make one art? It can only make one joke—one Theatre. Things which slowly, by a natural law join together, may have some right in the course of many years or many centuries to ask Nature to bestow a new name on their product. Only by this means can a new art be born. I do not believe that the old mother approves of the forcing process; and if she ever winks at it, she soon has her revenge; and so it is with the arts. You cannot commingle them and cry out that you have created a new art. *If you can find in Nature a new material, one which has never yet been used by man to give form to his thoughts, then you can say that you are on the high road towards creating a new art. For you have found that by which you can create it.* It then only remains for you to begin. The Theatre, as I see it, has yet to find that material." And thus their conversation ends.

For my part I am with the artist's last statement. My pleasure shall not be to compete with the strenuous photographer, and I shall ever aim to get something entirely opposed to life as we see it. This flesh-and-blood life, lovely as it is to us all, is for me not a thing made to search into, or to give out again to the world, even conventionalized. I think that my aim shall rather be to catch some far-off glimpse of that spirit which we call Death—to recall beautiful things from the imaginary world; they say they are cold, these dead things, I do not know—they often seem warmer and more living than that which parades as life. Shades—spirits seem to me to be more beautiful, and filled with more vitality than men and women; cities of men and women packed with pettiness, creatures inhuman, secret, coldest cold, hardest humanity. For, looking too long upon life, may one not find all this to be not the beautiful, nor the mysterious, nor the tragic, but the dull, the melodramatic, and the silly: the conspiracy against vitality—against both red heat and white heat? And from such things which lack the sun of life it is not possible to draw inspiration. But from that mysterious, joyous, and superbly complete life which is called Death—that life of shadow and of unknown shapes, where all cannot be blackness and fog as is supposed, but vivid colour, vivid light, sharp-cut form; and which one finds peopled with strange, fierce and solemn figures, pretty figures and calm figures, and those figures impelled to some wondrous harmony of movement—all this is something more than a mere matter of fact. From this idea of death, which seems a kind of spring, a blossoming—from this land and from this idea can come so vast an inspiration, that with unhesitating exultation I leap forward to it; and behold, in an instant, I find my arms full of flowers. I advance but a pace or two and again plenty is around me. I pass at ease on a sea of beauty, I sail whither the winds take me—*there*, there is no danger. So much for my own personal wish; but the entire Theatre of the world is not represented in me, nor in a hundred artists or actors, but in something far different. Therefore what my personal aim may be is of very little importance. Yet the aim of the Theatre as a whole is to restore its art, and it should commence by banishing from the Theatre this idea of impersonation, this idea of reproducing Nature; for, while impersonation is in the Theatre, the Theatre can never become free. The performers should train under the influence of an earlier teaching (if the very earliest and finest principles are too stern to commence with), and they will have to avoid that frantic desire to put *life* into their work; for three thousand times against one time it means the bringing of excessive gesture, swift mimicry, speech which bellows and scene which dazzles, on to the stage, in the wild and vain belief that by such means vitality can be conjured there. And in a few instances, to prove the rule, all this partially succeeds. It succeeds partially with the bubbling personalities of the Stage. With them it is a case of sheer triumph *in spite* of the rules, in the very teeth of the rules, and we who look on throw our hats into the air, cheer, and cheer again. *We have to*; we don't want to consider or to question; we go with the tide through admiration and suggestion. That we are hypnotized our taste cares not a rap: we are delighted to be so moved, and we literally jump for joy. The great personality has triumphed both over us and the art. But personalities such as these are extremely rare, and if we wish to see a personality assert itself in the Theatre and entirely triumph as an actor we must at the same time be quite indifferent about the play and the other actors, about beauty and art.

Those who do not think with me in this whole matter are the worshippers, or respectful admirers, of the personalities of the Stage. It is intolerable to them that I should assert that the Stage must be cleared of all its actors and actresses before it will again revive. How could they agree with me? That would include the removal of their favourites—the two or three beings who transform the stage for them from a vulgar joke into an ideal land. But what should they fear? No danger threatens their favourites—for were it possible to put an act into force to prohibit all men and women from appearing before the public upon the stage of a theatre, this would not in the least affect these favourites—these men and women of personality whom the playgoers crown. Consider any one of these personalities born at a period when the Stage was unknown; would it in any way have lessened their power—hindered their expression? Not a whit. Personality invents the means and ways by which it shall express itself; and acting is but one—the very least—of the means at the command of a great personality, and these men and women would have been famous at any time, and in any calling. But if there are many to whom it is intolerable that I should propose to clear the Stage of ALL the actors and actresses in order to revive the Art of the Theatre, there are others to whom it seems agreeable.

"The artist," says Flaubert, "should be in his work like God in creation, invisible and all-powerful; he should be felt everywhere and seen nowhere. Art should be raised above personal affection and nervous susceptibility. It is time to give it the perfection of the physical sciences by means of a pitiless method." And again, "I have always tried not to belittle Art for the satisfaction of an isolated personality." He is thinking mainly of the art of literature; but if he feels this so strongly of the writer, one who is never actually seen, but merely stands half revealed behind his work, how totally opposed must he have been to the actual appearance of the actor—personality or no personality.

Charles Lamb says: "To see Lear acted, to see an old man tottering about with a stick, turned out of doors by his daughters on a rainy night, has nothing in it but what is painful and disgusting. We want to take him in to shelter, that is all the feeling the acting of Lear ever produced in me. The contemptible machinery by which they mimic the storm which he goes in is not more inadequate to represent the horror of the real elements than any actor can be to represent Lear. They might more easily propose to personate the Satan of Milton upon a stage, or one of Michelangelo's terrible figures—Lear is essentially impossible to be represented on the stage."

"Hamlet himself seems hardly capable of being acted," says William Hazlitt.

Dante in *La Vita Nuova* tells us that, in a dream, Love, in the figure of a youth, appeared to him. Discoursing of Beatrice, Dante is told by Love "to compose certain things in rhyme, in the which thou shalt set forth how strong a mastership I have obtained over thee, through her. And so write these things that they shall seem rather to be spoken by a third person, and not directly by thee to her, which is scarce fitting." And again: "There came upon me a great desire to say somewhat in rhyme: but when I began thinking how I should say it, methought that to speak of her were unseemly, unless I spoke to other ladies in the second person." We see then that to these men it is wrong that the living person should advance into the frame and display himself upon his own canvas. They hold it as "unseemly"—"scarce fitting."

We have here witnesses against the whole

business of the modern stage. Collectively they pass the following sentence: That it is bad art to make so personal, so emotional, an appeal that the beholder forgets the thing itself while swamped by the personality, the emotion, of its maker. And now for the testimony of an actress.

Eleonora Duse has said: "To save the Theatre, the Theatre must be destroyed, the actors and actresses must all die of the plague. They poison the air, they make art impossible."[1]

We may believe her. She means what Flaubert and Dante mean, even if she words it differently. And there are many more witnesses to testify for me, if this is held to be insufficient evidence. There are the people who never go to the theatres, the millions of men against the thousands who do go. Then, we have the support of most of the managers of the Theatre of to-day. The modern theatre-manager thinks the stage should have its plays gorgeously decorated. He will say that no pains should be spared to bring every assistance towards cheating the audience into a sense of reality. He will never cease telling us how important all these decorations are. He urges all this for several reasons, and the following reason is not the least: He scents a grave danger in simple and good work; he sees that there is a body of people who are opposed to these lavish decorations; he knows that there has been a distinct movement in Europe

[1] *Studies in Seven Arts.* Arthur Symons. (Constable, 1900.)

against this display, it having been claimed that the great plays gained when represented in front of the plainest background. This movement can be proved to be a powerful one—it has spread from Krakau to Moscow, from Paris to Rome, from London to Berlin and Vienna. The managers see this danger ahead of them; they see that if once people came to realize this fact, if once the audience tasted of the delight which a sceneless play brings, they would then go further and desire the play which was presented without actors; and finally they would go on and on and on until *they*, and not the managers, had positively reformed the art.

Napoleon is reported to have said: "In life there is much that is unworthy which in art should be omitted; much of doubt and vacillation; and all should disappear in the representation of the hero. *We should see him as a statue in which the weakness and the tremors of the flesh are no longer perceptible.*" And not only Napoleon, but Ben Jonson, Lessing, Edmund Scherer, Hans Christian Andersen, Lamb, Goethe, George Sand, Coleridge, Anatole France, Ruskin, Pater,[1] and I suppose all the intelligent men

[1] Of Sculpture Pater writes: "Its white light, purged from the angry, bloodlike stains of action and passion, reveals, not what is accidental in man, but the god in him, as opposed to man's restless movement." Again: "The base of all artistic genius is the power of conceiving humanity in a new, striking, rejoicing way, of putting a happy world of its own construction in place of the meaner world of common days, of generating around itself an atmosphere with a novel power of refraction, selecting, transforming, recombining the images it transmits, according to the choice of the imaginative intellect." And

THE LANTERN BEARERS

A design for costume and lighting, not *for a modern theatre.*

[*Face page* 80.

and women of Europe—one does not speak of Asia, for even the unintelligent in Asia fail to comprehend photographs while understanding art as a simple and clear manifestation—have protested against this *reproduction* of Nature, and with it photographic and weak actuality. They have protested against all this, and the theatrical managers have argued against them energetically, and so we look for the truth to emerge in due time. It is a reasonable conclusion. Do away with the real tree, do away with the reality of delivery, do away with the reality of action, and you tend towards the doing away with the actor. This is what must come to pass in time, and I like to see the managers supporting the idea already. Do away with the actor, and you do away with the means by which a debased stage-realism is produced and flourishes. No longer would there be a living figure to confuse us into connecting actuality and art; no longer a living figure in which the weakness and tremors of the flesh were perceptible.

The actor must go, and in his place comes the inanimate figure—the Über-marionette we may call him, until he has won for himself a better name. Much has been written about the puppet, or marionette. There are some excellent volumes upon him, and he has also inspired several works of art. To-day

again: "All that is accidental, all that distracts the simple effect upon us of the supreme types of humanity, all traces in them of the commonness of the world, it gradually purges away."

in his least happy period many people come to regard him as rather a superior doll—and to think he has developed from the doll. This is incorrect. He is a descendant of the stone images of the old temples—he is to-day a rather degenerate form of a god. Always the close friend of children, he still knows how to select and attract his devotees.

When any one designs a puppet on paper, he draws a stiff and comic-looking thing. Such an one has not even perceived what is contained in the idea which we now call the marionette. He mistakes gravity of face and calmness of body for blank stupidity and angular deformity. Yet even modern puppets are extraordinary things. The applause may thunder or dribble, their hearts beat no faster, no slower, their signals do not grow hurried or confused; and, though drenched in a torrent of bouquets and love, the face of the leading lady remains as solemn, as beautiful and as remote as ever. There is something more than a flash of genius in the marionette, and there is something in him more than the flashiness of displayed personality. The marionette appears to me to be the last echo of some noble and beautiful art of a past civilization. But as with all art which has passed into fat or vulgar hands, the puppet has become a reproach. All puppets are now but low comedians.

They imitate the comedians of the larger and fuller blooded stage. They enter only to fall on their back. They drink only to reel, and make love only to raise a laugh. They have forgotten the counsel of their mother the Sphinx. Their bodies have lost their grave grace, they have become stiff. Their eyes have lost that infinite subtlety of seeming to sec; now they only stare. They display and jingle their wires and are cocksure in their wooden wisdom. They have failed to remember that their art should carry on it the same stamp of reserve that we see at times on the work of other artists, and that the highest art is that which conceals the craft and forgets the craftsman. Am I mistaken, or is it not the old Greek Traveller of 800 B.C. who, describing a visit to the temple-theatre in Thebes, tells us that he was won to their beauty by their "noble artificiality"? "Coming into the House of Visions I saw afar off the fair brown Queen seated upon her throne—her tomb—for both it seemed to me. I sank back upon my couch and watched her symbolic movements. With so much ease did her rhythms alter as with her movements they passed from limb to limb; with such a show of calm did she unloose for us the thoughts of her breast; so gravely and so beautifully did she linger on the statement of her sorrow, that with us it seemed as if no sorrow could harm her; no distortion of body or feature allowed us to dream that she was conquered; the passion and the pain were continually being caught by her hands, held gently, and viewed calmly. Her arms and hands seemed at one moment like a thin warm fountain of water which rose, then broke and fell with all those sweet pale fingers like spray into her lap. It would have been as a revelation of art to us had I not already seen that the same spirit dwelt in the other examples of the art of these Egyptians. This 'Art of Showing and Veiling,' as they call it, is so great a spiritual force in the land that it plays the larger part in their religion. We may learn from it somewhat of the power and the grace of courage, for it is impossible to witness a performance without a sense of physical and spiritual refreshment." This in 800 B.C. And who knows whether the puppet shall not once again become the faithful medium for the beautiful thoughts of the artist. May we not look forward with hope to that day which shall bring back to us once more the figure, or symbolic creature, made also by the cunning of the artist, so that we can gain once more the "noble artificiality" which the old writer speaks of? Then shall we no longer be under the cruel influence of the emotional confessions of weakness which are nightly witnessed by the people and which in their turn create in the beholders the very weaknesses which are exhibited. To that end we must study to remake these images—no longer content with a puppet, we must create an über-marionette. The über-marionette will not compete with life—rather will it go beyond it. Its ideal will not be the flesh and blood but rather the body in trance—it will aim to clothe itself with a death-like beauty while exhaling a living spirit. Several times in the course of this essay has a word or two about Death found its way on to the paper—called there by the incessant clamouring of "Life! Life! Life!" which the realists keep up. And this might be easily mistaken for an affectation, especially by those who have no sympathy or delight in the power and the mysterious joyousness which is in all passionless works of art. If the famous Rubens and the celebrated Raphael made none but passionate and exuberant statements, there were many artists before them and since to whom moderation in their art was the most precious of all their aims, and these more than all others exhibit the true masculine manner. The other flamboyant or drooping artists whose works and names catch the eye of to-day do not so much speak like men as bawl like animals, or lisp like women.

The wise, the moderate masters, strong because of the laws to which they swore to remain ever faithful—their names unknown for the most part—a fine family—the creators of the great and tiny gods of the East and the West, the guardians of those larger times: these all bent their thoughts forward towards the unknown, searching for sights and sounds in that peaceful and joyous country, that they might raise a figure of stone or sing a verse, investing it with that same peace and joy seen from afar, so as to balance all the grief and turmoil here.

In America we can picture these brothers of that family of masters, living in their superb ancient cities, colossal cities, which I ever think of as able to be moved in a single day; cities of spacious tents of silk and canopies of gold under which dwelt their gods; dwellings which contained all the requirements of the most fastidious; those moving cities which, as they travelled from height to plain, over rivers and down valleys, seemed like some vast advancing army of peace. And in each city not one or two men called "artists" whom the rest of the city looked upon as ne'er-do-well idlers, but many men chosen by the community because of their higher powers of perception—artists. For that is what the title of artist means: one who perceives more than his fellows, and who records more than he has seen. And not the least among those artists was the artist of the ceremonies, the creator of the visions, the minister whose duty it was to celebrate their guiding spirit—the spirit of Motion.

In Asia, too, the forgotten masters of the temples and all that those temples contained have permeated every thought, every mark, in their work with this sense of calm motion resembling death—glorifying and greeting it. In Africa (which some of us think we are but now to civilize) this spirit dwelt, the essence of the perfect civilization. There, too, dwelt the great masters, not individuals obsessed with the idea of each asserting his personality as if it were a valuable and mighty thing, but content because of a kind of holy patience to move their brains and their fingers only in that direction permitted by the law—in the service of the simple truths.

How stern the law was, and how little the artist of that day permitted himself to make an exhibition of his personal feelings, can be discovered by looking at any example of Egyptian art. Look at any limb ever carved by the Egyptians, search into all those carved eyes, they will deny you until the crack of doom. Their attitude is so silent that it is death-like. Yet tenderness is there, and charm is there; prettiness is even there side by side with the force; and love bathes each single work; but gush, emotion, swaggering personality of the artist ?—not one single breath of it. Fierce doubts of hope ?—not one hint of such a thing. Strenuous determination ?—not a sign of it has escaped the artist; none of these confessions—stupidities. Nor pride, nor fear, nor the comic, nor any indication that the artist's mind or hand was for the thousandth part of a moment out of the command of the laws which ruled him. How superb! This it is to be a great artist; and the amount of emotional outpourings of to-day and of yesterday are no signs of supreme intelligence, that is to say, are no signs of supreme art. To

Europe came this spirit, hovered over Greece, could hardly be driven out of Italy, but finally fled, leaving a little stream of tears—pearls—before us. And we, having crushed most of them, munching them along with the acorns of our food, have gone farther and fared worse, and have prostrated ourselves before the so-called "great masters," and have worshipped these dangerous and flamboyant personalities. On an evil day we thought in our ignorance that it was us they were sent to draw; that it was our thoughts they were sent to express; that it was something to do with us that they were putting into their architecture, their music. And so it was we came to demand that we should be able to recognize ourselves in all that they put hand to; that is to say, in their architecture, in their sculpture, in their music, in their painting, and in their poetry we were to figure—and we also reminded them to invite us with the familiar words: "Come as you are."

The artists after many centuries have given in, that which we asked them for they have supplied. And so it came about that when this ignorance had driven off the fair spirit which once controlled the mind and hand of the artist, a dark spirit took its place; the happy-go-lucky hooligan in the seat of the law—that is to say, a stupid spirit reigning; and everybody began to shout about Renaissance! while all the time the painters, musicians, sculptors, architects, vied one with the other to supply the demand—that all these things should be so made that all people could recognize them as having something to do with themselves.

Up sprang portraits with flushed faces, eyes which bulged, mouths which leered, fingers itching to come out of their frames, wrists which exposed the pulse; all the colours higgledy-piggledy; all the lines in hubbub, like the ravings of lunacy. Form breaks into panic; the calm and cool whisper of life in trance which once had breathed out such an ineffable hope is heated, fired into a blaze and destroyed, and in its place—*realism*, the blunt statement of life, something everybody misunderstands while recognizing. And all far from the purpose of art: for its purpose is not to reflect the actual facts of this life, because it is not the custom of the artist to walk behind things, having won it as his privilege to walk in front of them—to lead. Rather should life reflect the likeness of the spirit, for it was the spirit which first chose the artist to chronicle its beauty.[1] And in that picture, if the form be that of the living, on account of its beauty and tenderness, the colour for it must be sought from that unknown land of the imagination, and what is that but the land where dwells that which we call Death? So it is not lightly and flippantly that I speak of puppets and their power to retain the beautiful and remote expressions in

[1] "All forms are perfect in the poet's mind: but these are not abstracted or compounded from Nature; they are from Imagination."—William Blake.

form and face even when subjected to a patter of praise, a torrent of applause. There are persons who have made a jest of these puppets. "Puppet is a term of contempt, though there still remain some who find beauty in these little figures, degenerate though they have become.

To speak of a puppet with most men and women is to cause them to giggle. They think at once of the wires; they think of the stiff hands and the jerky movements; they tell me it is "a funny little doll." But let me tell them a few things about these puppets. Let me again repeat that they are the descendants of a great and noble family of Images, images which were indeed made "in the likeness of God;" and that many centuries ago these figures had a rhythmical movement and not a jerky one; had no need for wires to support them, nor did they speak through the nose of the hidden manipulator. [Poor Punch, I mean no slight to you! You stand alone, dignified in your despair, as you look back across the centuries with painted tears still wet upon your ancient cheeks, and you seem to cry out appealingly to your dog: "Sister Anne, Sister Anne, is *nobody* coming?" And then with that superb bravado of yours, you turn the force of our laughter (and my tears) upon yourself with the heartrending shriek of "Oh my nose! Oh my nose! Oh my nose!"] Did you think, ladies and gentlemen, that these puppets were always little things of but a foot high?

Indeed, no! The puppet had once a more generous form than yourselves.

Do you think that he kicked his feet about on a little platform six feet square, made to resemble a little old-fashioned theatre, so that his head almost touched the top of the proscenium? and do you think that he always lived in a little house where the door and windows were as small as a doll's house, with painted window-blinds parted in the centre, and where the flowers of his little garden had courageous petals as big as his head? Try and dispel this idea altogether from your minds, and let me tell you something of his habitation.

In Asia lay his first kingdom. On the banks of the Ganges they built him his home, a vast palace springing from column to column into the air and pouring from column to column down again into the water. Surrounded by gardens spread warm and rich with flowers and cooled by fountains; gardens into which no sounds entered, in which hardly anything stirred. Only in the cool and private chambers of this palace the swift minds of his attendants stirred incessantly. Something they were making which should become him, something to honour the spirit which had given him birth. And then, one day, the ceremony.

In this ceremony he took part; a celebration once more in praise of the Creation; the old thanksgiving, the hurrah for existence, and with it the sterner hurrah for the privilege of the existence to come, which is veiled by the word Death. And during this ceremony there appeared before the eyes of the brown worshippers the symbols of all things on earth and in Nirvana. The symbol of the beautiful tree, the symbol of the hills, the symbols of those rich ores which the hills contained; the symbol of the cloud, of the wind, and of all swift moving things; the symbol of the quickest of moving things, of thought, of remembrance; the symbol of the animal, the symbol of Buddha and of Man—and here he comes, the figure, the puppet at whom you all laugh so much. You laugh at him to-day because none but his weaknesses are left to him. He reflects these from you; but you would not have laughed had you seen him in his prime, in that age when he was called upon to be the symbol of man in the great ceremony, and, stepping forward, was the beautiful figure of our heart's delight. If we should laugh at and insult the memory of the puppet, we should be laughing at the fall that we have brought about in ourselves—laughing at the beliefs and images we have broken. A few centuries later, and we find his home a little the worse for wear. From a temple, it has become, I will not say a theatre, but something between a temple and a theatre, and he is losing his health in it. Something is in the air; his doctors tell him he must be careful. "And what am I to fear most?" he asks them. They answer him: "Fear most the vanity of men." He thinks: "But that is what I myself have always taught, that we who celebrated in joy this our existence, should have this one great fear. Is it possible that I, one who has ever revealed this truth, should be one to lose sight of it and should myself be one of the first to fall ? Clearly some subtle attack is to be made on me. I will keep my eyes upon the heavens." And he dismisses his doctors and ponders upon it.

And now let me tell you who it was that came to disturb the calm air which surrounded this curiously perfect thing. It is on record that somewhat later he took up his abode on the Far Eastern coast, and there came two women to look upon him. And at the ceremony to which they came he glowed with such earthly splendour and yet such unearthly simplicity, that though he prove an inspiration to the thousand nine hundred and ninety-eight souls who participated in the festival, an inspiration which cleared the mind even as it intoxicated, yet to these two women it proved an intoxication only. He did not see them, his eyes were fixed on the heavens; but he charged them full of a desire too great to be quenched; the desire to stand as the direct symbol of the divinity in man. No sooner thought than done; and arraying themselves as best they could in garments (" like his " they thought), moving with gestures (" like his " they said) and being able to cause wonderment in the minds of the beholders (" even as he does " they cried), they built themselves a temple (" like his," " like his "), and supplied the demand of the vulgar, the whole thing a poor parody.

This is on record. It is the first record in the East of the actor. The actor springs from the foolish vanity of two women who were not strong enough to look upon the symbol of godhead without desiring to tamper with it; and the parody proved profitable. In fifty or a hundred years places for such parodies were to be found in all parts of the land.

Weeds, they say, grow quickly, and that wilderness of weeds, the modern theatre, soon sprang up. The figure of the divine puppet attracted fewer and fewer lovers, and the women were quite the latest thing. With the fading of the puppet and the advance of these women who exhibited themselves on the stage in his place, came that darker spirit which is called Chaos, and in its wake the triumph of the riotous personality. Do you see, then, what has made me love and learn to value that which to-day we call the "puppet" and to detest that which we call "life" in art? I pray earnestly for the return of the image—the über-marionette to the Theatre; and when he comes again and is but seen, he will be loved so well that once more will it be possible for the people to return to their ancient joy in ceremonies—once more will Creation be celebrated—homage rendered to existence—and divine and happy intercession made to Death.

FLORENCE: *March* 1907.

SOME EVIL TENDENCIES OF THE MODERN THEATRE

AS I step before you to speak about the Theatre do not mistake me as a reformer. I beg of you do not do that. When I become a reformer—that is to say, a surgeon and a physician in one—I shall take Hamlet's advice and "reform it altogether," beginning with myself and ending with the limelight man.

But to be a reformer one must be in the position of a reformer; that is to say, one must have at least half-a-dozen or a dozen theatres in different parts of the world, so that the reforms spread evenly. Two small progressive theatres in Paris, London or Berlin are quite useless towards improving the state of things in the Theatre, its state as an art and an institution. Those who live in London or Berlin know very little what is passing in the two French theatres. Those who live in Paris and London have seldom heard of the Berlin theatres. And those who live in Berlin and Paris hardly know that any such theatres exist in England. And so it is that these gallant little theatres, which make daily efforts to improve the state of things, bring about no marked nor lasting improvement, because all their energy and occasional good deeds evaporate after a few thousand people have left the theatre. And the Art of the Theatre still remains unknown.

It would be quite another matter (and I should be unable to write as I do) if any of these theatres had discovered *Laws* for the Art of the Theatre; for these theatres to be unknown, unheard of, would matter but little to the men who are busy all the time searching for the truths which are the basis of all things. One of the evil tendencies of the modern theatre is to forget this entirely, to aim at being heard of for a few days and months, to make an effort in front of a full audience for two or three hundred evenings, and there an end. To reform this would it not need the headlong strength of some profoundly stupid giant ?

I write, then, as an onlooker, not as a casual onlooker nor as an irritable one, but more as one who takes a loving interest in watching the growth of plants in a beautiful garden. The eye of such a man is instantly arrested by the weeds. Nothing seems so foolish or so abominable to him as the weeds which absorb the goodness from the soil, robbing the other plants of that goodness and altogether spoiling the beauty of the garden; and it is the weeds, the evil tendencies of the modern theatre, that I am concerned with here.

Bear in mind that when I speak of the Theatre I do not allude especially to what is called the English theatre; nor do I mean that which they call the French theatre; I do not particularly mean what is called the German theatre, nor the Italian, Scandinavian nor Russian theatres. All theatres of all lands are alike in all things except language, and, alas! the weeds so closely resemble each other that it is positively comic.

I speak then of the Theatre as a whole, the Theatre of Europe and America, for I have seen none other; though I believe, from what I hear, that the Eastern Theatre abstains from offending the intelligence.

The tendency of the Western Theatre is to disregard the vital principles of the art: To invent or borrow with haste so-called reforms which may attract the public, not those which are necessary to the health of the art: To encourage piracy and imitation instead of cultivating natural resource: To take the keys of the place from their rightful keepers, the artists, and to hand them over to the "business man" or anyone.

I write, as I say, as an onlooker, but I have been for over fifteen years a worker in the theatre. This I say for the benefit of those who may not know, and who question my authority for these statements.

I have many times written that there is only one way to obtain unity in the Art of the Theatre. I suppose it is unnecessary to explain why unity should be there as in other great arts; I suppose it offends no one to admit that unless unity reigns "chaos is come again; I suppose this *is* quite clear;—?—! Very well, then. So far, so good. And it should not be difficult to make clear how this unity is to be obtained. I have attempted this in my book, *The Art of the Theatre*,[1] and now I wish to make clear by what process unity is lost.

Let me make a list (an incomplete one, but it will serve) of the different workers in the theatre. When I have made this list I will tell you how many are head-cooks and how they assist in the spoiling of the broth.

First and foremost, there is the proprietor of the theatre. Secondly, there is the business manager who rents the theatre. Thirdly, there is the stage-director, sometimes three or four of these. There are also three or four business men. Then we come to the chief actor and the chief actress. Then we have the actor and the actress who are next to the chief; that is to say, who are ready to step into their places if required. Then there are from twenty to sixty other actors and actresses. Besides this, there is a gentleman who designs scenes. Another who designs costumes. A third who devotes his time to arranging lights. A fourth who attends to the machinery (generally the hardest worker in the theatre). And then we have from twenty to a hundred under-workers, scene-painters, costume makers, limelight manipulators, dressers, scene-shifters, under machinists, extra ladies and gentlemen, cleaners, programme sellers: and there we have the bunch.

Now look carefully at this list. We see seven

[1] See page 137.

heads and two very influential members. Seven directors instead of one, and nine opinions instead of one.

Now, then, it is impossible for a work of art ever to be produced where more than one brain is permitted to direct; and if works of art are not seen in the Theatre this one reason is a sufficient one, though there are plenty more.

Do you wish to know why there are seven masters instead of one? It is because there is no one man in the theatre who is a master in himself, that is to say, there is no one man capable of inventing and rehearsing a play: capable of designing and superintending the construction of both scenery and costume: of writing any necessary music: of inventing such machinery as is needed and the lighting that is to be used.

No manager of a theatre has made these things his study; and it is a disgrace to the Western Theatre that this statement can be made. You have but to ask any manager in London, Berlin or Paris whether he can invent the drama which is to be presented in his theatre. Or ask him whether he can invent and design the scenes which are to be shown on his stage. Or ask him whether he knows anything about historic or imaginative costume; and whether he knows a beautiful colour from an ugly one. Whether he can even combine lovely tones and colours together so as to form a whole, and whether he knows anything of the hand, the wrist, the arm, the neck, and all the rest of the values of the body in movement. Ask him whether he knows how much light is sufficient to fully illumine twenty cubic feet, and how much will *over*-light twenty cubic feet and so waste the light. Ask him if he knows the weight of wood and cloth, or if he can tell you how swiftly or how slowly a stage floor is able to be raised or lowered. Ask him any of these things, and he will blandly tell you (with shame be it spoken) *that it is not his business.* And then this remarkable master of the Art of the Theatre will call up his co-workers, and, pointing to them, he will say, "These are my assistants."

He is not speaking the truth. They are not his assistants, they are his masters. They lead him with a hook in his nose like the great Leviathan which we see in pictures of the older day pageants. He looks mighty terrible, but he is only made of emptiness covered with paste-board. Is not this a fine master? Is not this a pretty way to obtain this same unity, this one thing vital to the art?

So then we have to turn to the six other masters, each of whom helps towards the patchwork, and see if they will help us to a reasonable answer. The *régisseur*, or stage-manager, is under the delusion that in truth he is the one who is the artist, the inventor, the master, but, poor fellow, he is nothing of the kind, for no one is the master: each throwing into the broth whatever ingredient he will. All are petty masters, each hindering the other. Many of the régisseurs, or stage-managers, are known to me. I have worked with some; others I have spoken with; but all are under the delusion that I mention. It is a kind of delusion of despair, for régisseurs are really very good workers and spare themselves no pains when they are in the theatre. They should have spared no pains to prepare themselves for their task *before* entering the theatre.

As our questions to the director of the theatre met with such a lamentable reply, let us see whether the régisseur, or stage-manager, will be able to give us a better answer. Let us ask him, let us ask any régisseur in Europe or America, if he can imagine and invent that which is to be presented to the audience; that is to say, the piece, the play, the idea, or whatever you may call it. Let us ask him whether he can design the scenes and costumes for that piece, and whether he can superintend their construction—that is to say, whether he knows the secrets of line and colour and their manipulation. Let us ask him whether he can direct without the aid of experts the different workmen who are employed on account of their utility, not on account of their imagination. And if there is *one* such man in Europe or America who can reply "Yes" to all these questions, he is the man to whom the control of the stages of Europe and America should be offered; for such a man would be able to acquire the same capacities as himself, for he would know what was necessary. And when you have ten such men in Europe you have a new Theatre. But there are not ten, as you will find out if you ask. I could not tell you the name of one.

And so it is that unity, as I have said, is absent from the Art of the Theatre.

Yet there are several brains in the theatre who know that if they could find the secret which would produce this unity they would have discovered a very good deed. In Germany there are a few such men searching in the topmost branches of the tree. But, as they do not think to search at the roots, their search leads them into strange acts. They mean very well, but they act very queerly. They are red-hot in the pursuit, but they run blindfold.

The tendency of these men is to borrow. They borrow from every conceivable source. They borrow from the painters, they borrow from the architects, they even borrow from their own fellows, any idea, so long as it is attractive; and so long as the idea has a plain enough base on which to build a little structure of sense, it is quickly transferred into the theatre.

What a way for one who wishes to be called an artist to act! Clever artists illustrating week after week in the comic papers of Germany find their ideas seized on and thrust upon the stage of the *modern* theatre. "Jugend" decorates Shakespeare and Bernard Shaw, and "Simplicissimus" is useful for Gorky and Wedekind.

These things are experimental and rash innovations, dangerous alike to the art and to the public. Hastiness characterizes all things in the theatre of to-day; hasty reforms, hasty preparation, hasty ideas as hastily carried out. The directors show an eagerness to-day to secure the studio painters to design scenes for them.

How strange this is! Do they not see that they are inviting into their theatre that which in time will turn and rend it asunder, adding a fresh wound to an already mutilated corpse?

Do they not also see that to invite the studio painters into the theatre is an insult to those scene-painters whose families have worked in the theatre for hundreds of years? and do they not also see that the peculiar merit of the studio painter is of no avail inside a theatre, and that to engage a man who paints the side of a house would be a shrewder act on their part? One curious side of this question of the painter being invited to co-operate in the theatre is that I am looked on as supporting the tendency, and, in fact, am pointed out as an example of the success which attends the movement, whereas I am against the whole thing from beginning to end.

If the painter could bring any release for the art which lies so bound, firstly by convention, secondly by the unintelligence and incapacity of those who are supposed to be its *masters* (?), then their coming would be a welcome thing; but it is not release they bring; they bring one more fetter. It is not their fault to offer their service; it is our fault to accept it. We borrow and we borrow and we borrow. We are already so much in debt that we are nearly in despair. And we are in such haste. Why, this even makes the borrowing careless. The bad is copied as swiftly and as thoughtlessly as the good. Any picture, any design, provided it is flashy enough or eccentric enough, is seized on by these hasty and thoughtless directors and régisseurs, squeezed, and its juice, bitter or sweet, extracted from it. Yet this hurrying and blundering is not so strange, after all, and any one who has lived a year in a theatre can understand it. Day—afternoon—evening—night: these gentlemen of the theatre are continually on the rush. (I am speaking of the *modern* theatres; which are supposed to be in the advance.) Rehearsing in the morning, seeing people in the midday, studying parts, looking at scenery, play reading, attending receptions, an author to see, a critic to entertain, an artist to catch, incessant quarrels to smooth over, at least one new play to be brought out each month, capital to find, building to superintend, always one incessant hustle.

Where, then, is the time to stop and consider about the *art* of the thing? This may do very well for an oil business or a large grocery; these things *thrive* by hustling: not so an art. In this haste all

JULIUS CAESAR

ACT III. SCENE II.

THE FORUM.

Here we see Mark Antony addressing half Rome. A hundred thousand citizens are seen at the back; Mark Antony leans towards them and away from us, and you hear his shrill, high voice. In the front, nearest us, there is silence. There the conspirators wait.

There is no example of Roman architecture here, for Shakespeare never insists on accuracy of detail. Besides, who knows now what the Forum looked like, so why attempt to be accurate about the Past when to be so is impossible ?

All I felt was the crowd, and the two parties. I had to bring all these in and divide them so that we should feel the divisions clearly. I put the crowd farthest off because, although a hundred thousand voices can drown one voice when it is between you and the speaker, still, a hundred thousand voices make an excellent background to the voice of a personality. For instance, I never knew distant thunder, however mighty it was, to interrupt a conversation.

The man who is persuading the crowd is in the middle distance.
Those against whom he is persuading them are in the foreground.
Then silence can be felt.

[*Face page* 104.

thought of the principles or the beauty of the art is lost sight of and all desire to produce beauty departs.

After all, we must admit that beauty by the side of intrigue is but a poor sort of a thing to follow; and a sort of burlesque intrigue is the goddess of the theatre of to-day. Burlesque intrigue, that is exactly the class of diplomacy in the theatre, and how seriously these little imitation diplomatists go about their work!

It is very curious to read in De Goncourt's *Memoirs* of the impression the two brothers received when they wished to honour the theatre by bringing their work on to its stage. Edmond de Goncourt, a true courtier of distinction, surrounded by these burlesque diplomatists of the theatre, what a picture he paints for us! How keenly we feel, when reading the account of his different interviews with these gentlemen, how vulgar and contemptible the situation must have been.

It horrifies and disgusts me to think that for ever and for ever and for ever such men as De Goncourt, De Musset, Victor Hugo, Dumas, Goethe, Browning, and all the great writers and all the men of truest distinction in the world should be put in such a humiliating position; and not only is it *that* which disgusts me, but it is shameful that it is ever the Theatre which should put these men in this position. Must the Theatre continually cry out that it contains none but the fifth-rate men? Must the men of the theatre continually *act* when in the presence of other artists? And if they act, must they for ever continue to act ignominiously, so that the whole world cries out: "Behold an actor, and a damn bad actor into the bargain!" The actor has lately been priding himself that he has raised himself from the old position when he was held as a vagabond and a thief. This is especially the case in England. Would to goodness that he had remained a vagabond and a thief, so that he had not lost his distinction; for to become a gentleman in name, but grow vulgar to the core, is to be many times worse than a vagabond and a thief.

Let the Theatre drop its stupid games of amateur diplomacy. When it does its work itself there will be no longer need for anything of the kind. When it drops this bad habit it will have time to attend to the things which are of more importance, and it will have then the spirit to look at things squarely.

But, now, to return to the tendency to invite the painters and other artists to assist us in our work, and the haste which characterizes everything we do. These two tendencies have driven the best workers out of the theatre. Century after century the artists of the theatre, despairing of ever seeing the stage awaken from its state of drunken lethargy, depart from the theatre and go elsewhere.

The result is that to-day there are no more artists in the theatre. The heads of the theatre are always men with a certain amount of business capacity; we may, in fact, call them business men.

The business man employs one or two people who know what a tree looks like as distinguished from a cat, and of course that is very useful. And so when the business man wants a tree his workman brings him one. How simple! When he wants a forest, say, in *A Midsummer Night's Dream*, his man brings him one. He does not paint one, of course not! That would be risky; risky and difficult. No, he has asked for a forest, and his man brings him the real and original thing, tree by tree. "There you are, Mr. Manager, there's your forest for you," and Mr. Manager replies, "By Jingo, so it is! What a magnificent artist you are!" And then he runs out into the highways and byways, having first put on his celluloid cuffs, and says to all his relations and customers: "Walk up, gentlemen! come and look at the scene which I have prepared for you! Have you ever seen a scene like that? I flatter myself that Nature can't do better." And his customers gasp. They gasp at the innocence of the man. All they can politely say to him is: "It is very realistic"! And so through this crass innocence, realism reigns in the theatre, for the people are ever polite.

Not only does the manager demand a forest and is supplied with one, but he says to his actors: "Why don't you walk about and talk like ordinary beings? Be natural! Be natural! Be natural!" And he will applaud any little mistake like tripping over the carpet, or falling off a chair, if it is an accident, and will say: "Oh! capital! capital! that's most natural! Put that in every evening." Anything to get a sense of chance there. The idea of make-believe seems to him a preposterous idea when he can get the real thing. In England when he wants an army he sends one of his assistants to bring him half-a-dozen men from the so-and-so regiment and puts them into the armour of the Barusch period. He never thinks of training all his men to *appear* military as soldiers *are*. He doesn't reason in that way at all, but keeps on repeating: "What's the good of imitation when you can get the real article?"

And what is the good *if you want the real article?* Realism does want the real article, and art has nothing whatever to do with realism. There are people who hold that realism on the stage is not the bringing of real things in front of you. If it is not this, what is it?

Let us try to state. Let us say that when we make a realistic production we aim to put into a semi-real shape that which is already quite real. We aim to invest it with something lifelike, so that it appears to have a pulse in it, flesh and blood, and to possess other actual qualities. And now one turns to the real thing to find what we have to copy. We gaze long at a face. We see it is not beautiful, that it is not strong, that it is not healthy, and that it is everything which art detests. We look closely at a tree. We see it is in decay, that the leaves are falling, that it is half a skeleton. We look carefully at a building, we are struck by the quantity of bricks used and overcome by the thought of the labour and pain it must have cost to put all the bricks in the right place. And so we find that to look closely at reality is to be terrified by what we see; and, if not terrified, saddened. How unreasonable it is to say that the artist exists to copy the defects and blemishes of Nature! How ridiculous to say that man is gifted with vision in order to chronicle faults! To say that faults are beautiful and defects are charming is a platitude. They may or may not be, but not in art. Do they, perhaps, make a work of art more *interesting?* I think not. One may say only that they are a trifle comic, and that is all. And so in time realism produces and ends in the comic—realism is caricature. The theatre, with its realism, will end in the music-hall, for realism cannot go upwards, but always tends downwards. Down it goes until we reach the depths. And then, *Anarchy!* Ariel is destroyed and Caliban reigns.

And I do not really believe there is very much to be done; not that I am at all a pessimist in regard to the art, because I know well enough that this will emerge unaided in due time; but there is not very much to be done at present by the people who are now in power, for if they began "doing things" they would probably only make matters worse instead of better. Affectation would be added to vulgarity.

Something may be done by the younger men, but

not if they are under the influence of their elders, because then you get an old young man. Something is being done in England at the miniature Court Theatre, but the influence of the author is too strong there, an author who uses the theatre for purposes of *réclame.* Something is being done in the Deutches Theater in Berlin, but the influence of Jugend and Simplicissimus and Business men is too throng there. Besides, that theatre shows signs of the borrowing fever at a dreadfully high temperature. Then there is also the little Art Theatre in Moscow; full of energy, loving realism so well that they even turn realism itself into a joke. Then there is Antoine's Theatre and the Theatre des Arts, the two solitary efforts of Paris; but how little is achieved can be gauged by some of the last productions there.

If all these little theatres were moving forward in the same direction, all of them having one common idea and following one code of *laws*, then some little good might be expected, because they would all be in unison and in harmony; and the old-fashioned theatre with its plays and its scenery and its real actors would certainly be improved.

To expect what *ought* to happen, to expect the managers of these theatres to meet in council and to take an oath of allegiance to serve no other Muse but the Muse of *their* art, no longer to remain in bondage to the Muse of Literature or Painting, but to strike the first new note in honour of their own

Goddess, this ideal hope can only remain a dream, for man is vain and selfish; and besides, the Laws of the Art have not been inscribed. And it is because of this, because the Laws have not been inscribed, because neither the priests nor the worshippers know the Laws, *that all action is useless at present.* The Laws must be discovered and recorded. Not what each of us personally takes to be the law, but what it actually is. We can come to no disappointment by finding out. If all of us fail to find the thing and one comes along who makes it clear, who will there be to deny him ? The worst of it is that no one wants to find the law nowadays, but everyone wants to force his own ideas, trumpery or the reverse, upon the rest, or to make money. A great vanity and a petty selfishness tie our tongues and our brains.

What the Art of the Theatre (or rather we must call it the *Work* of the Theatre at present) lacks is *form.* It spreads, it wanders, it has no form. It is this which makes the difference between the work of the Theatre and the fine arts. To say that it lacks form is to say that it lacks beauty. In art, where there is no form there can be no beauty.

How then can it obtain this form ? Only by developing slowly under the laws. And these laws ? I have searched for them, and I believe I am finding some of them.

1908.

PLAYS AND PLAYWRIGHTS PICTURES AND PAINTERS IN THE THEATRE

WHEREVER I go and however intelligent or unintelligent the people may be, and however carefully they have read what I have written upon the Theatre, the eternal question comes back over and over again—sometimes aggressively put to one, sometimes nicely put: "Do you want to sweep away all the plays out of the theatre? Do you find the idea of the poet in the theatre offensive? Please say what is the meaning of this extraordinary idea of yours, that that which has been good for hundreds of years is suddenly to be held as bad." It is exceedingly difficult to reply to all this, and as it is exceedingly difficult let us try to do so.

Of course to me the whole question is so clear that it ceases to be a question any longer. It has become the obvious with me that when a man sets his hand to a work he should not take by the wrist another man's hand and use it to do the work in question, and then call it *his* work.

The whole thing is so obvious to me that, in order to be able to reply carefully and sensibly to those to whom it is not obvious, I must remove myself from the picture before me, and see every line in the pictures which the others see. And if I try to

"HUNGER." A Drama

Scene I.—The Servants.

I have another design for this Drama in another place in this book, and have written there all that is necessary concerning it. *(See illustration facing page 262).*

[*Face page* 112.

do that I shall have to see some very dull things, and discuss some very dull points, which are obvious to most of us ; but if the question has to be gone into at all perhaps this is inevitable.

I have a horrible dread of proving people to be wrong, especially the man who takes the arts easily. I have more than a large appreciation of his good sense. Besides, I do not want to prove that the man who goes to the pit to see *Richard the Third* is wrong for going there, no matter what his reason is.

Let us take the whole front row of the London pit, consisting of twenty people.

Ask them the reason why they have come to the theatre. Five reply, " I come to see Mr. —— act." Three reply, " It is such a great play, I like to hear it so much." Two giggle and reply, " We don't know why we come, but we think it is such fun." Two are there from a sense of duty both to the actors of the play and to the audience; and the other eight will give us several elaborate and conflicting reasons for their presence.

One will say, that it is the extraordinary sense of the impossible, the grim absurdity of the whole thing, which fascinates him. (Excellent judge !)

The second will tell you that, after having spent the day among dull and matter-of-fact people, it is quite interesting to find a body of people who will sit still while actors and scenery are pretending on the stage.

Then there is the third, the critical man ; one who having read how Edmund Kean illuminated Shakespeare by sudden flashes of genius, and that the Kemble family were of the "classical" school, and that Charles Fechter was a romantic actor; and having read a history of the stage which skips over the first couple of thousand years in two pages and only begins to go into detail when it comes to the Shakespearean era—this man will be there, because somehow he feels that the thing would be incomplete without him; he is one of the men who know—has he not read all about it ?

Then next to him is sitting a young lady, who, with the intelligence which is natural in her sex, is ready to see *all* that is there and more (or less) if required; and yet indeed she leans towards the "more" and is ever the champion of the "more" when she finds it.

Next to her sits the grumbler, one who goes to a theatre because he must, and who, I believe, is always the one who is most deeply moved by what he sees. Yet when the curtain is once down he will tell you that was not the way to do it at all. "Why," he says, "the actors are so many sticks; nothing real about them." He draws our attention to the flapping scenery and grumbles about the incidental music which he says spoils the effect; and he detests all those flashing lights, which he says spoil the illusion. But what illusion is destroyed he is totally unable to define. The rest of the row say that it is very nice indeed, and they all applaud heartily, while he continues to grunt and mumble, and keeps on repeating that "that isn't the way to do it."

And so we see that very nearly each single man or woman is come there for a different purpose, sees the thing in a different light, and composes what we can term an "audience;" that is to say, a single idea—that audience which the actor always looks on as one man, and which we must accept as the "ideal spectator."

One thing is irrefutable. They cannot keep away from the theatre. And another thing which we must admit is this: that out of the twenty, fifteen have come to see something. I will even go so far as to say that the entire twenty have come to see something; because the first on our list, the first five who came to hear Shakespeare more or less admit that they came to see it performed, for had they wished they could have joined the many thousands who sit at home and read it silently, and in this way hear it in their mind's ear with all its amazing and wonderful accompaniment; or joined those who read it together in societies.

So we can say somewhat surely that all have come to *see* the play. This desire is as fierce as any in the nature of man. Only when seeing does a man thoroughly believe. There are innumerable proofs of this, and many will occur to you at this moment without my mentioning them. So now, it is reasonable to ask that that which the people desire, and go to the theatre to find, should be given to them.

They go to see something; they should be shown it. Only by showing them will they be satisfied. Therefore I hold that properly to satisfy their eye, and through that their being, we should not confuse them or confuse their sense of sight, which is most delicate, by pounding at the same time at their ears with music or with words, nor by attacking their minds with problems and shaking their bodies with passions.

Let us take something as an example of what I mean: that part in the play of *Macbeth* where he prepares to nerve himself to rob King Duncan of his life. He is roaming about in and out of the dark corridors of his castle. Behind him, like his shadow, a servant moves, they pass and repass a window, and I think I see him gazing out a long time towards the heath. He continues his prowling, and then rests upon a stone bench. The servant, holding a trembling light, looks at him, and he looks back again. Once more he begins to pace the corridor; he is afraid to be left alone. He thinks of his wife, then becomes more afraid of being left quite alone. . . . " Go, bid thy mistress, when my drink is ready, She strike upon the bell."

The servant departs. He continues to roam up and down. In his agitation the figure of his wife takes the place of his servant. He feels particularly fine; he has an audience; he seems to take courage and his desire warms in him. He will do it. The servant returns, startling him for an instant. "Get thee to bed." He watches the flame of the torch as it dwindles and dwindles, down the steps leading to the basement; a flame at first, it now became a streak—a streak.

"Is this a dagger that I see before me,
The handle toward my hand? Come, let me clutch thee:
I have thee not, and yet I see thee still.
Art thou not, fatal vision, sensible
To feeling as to sight? or art thou but
A dagger of the mind; a false creation
Proceeding from the heat-oppressèd brain?
I see thee yet, in form as palpable
As that which now I draw.
Thou marshall'st me the way that I was going,
And such an instrument I was to use.
Mine eyes are made the fools o' the other senses,
Or else worth all the rest. I see thee still;
And on thy blade and dudgeon gouts of blood
Which was not so before.—There's no such thing.
It is the bloody business, which informs
Thus to mine eyes.—Now o'er the one half world
Nature seems dead, and wicked dreams abuse
The curtain'd sleep; now witchcraft celebrates
Pale Hecate's offerings; and wither'd murder,
Alarum'd by his sentinel, the wolf,
Whose howl 's his watch, thus with his stealthy pace,
With Tarquin's ravishing strides, towards his design
Moves like a ghost.——Thou sure and firm-set earth,
Hear not my steps, which way they walk, for fear
The very stones prate on my whereabout,
And take the present horror from the time,
Which now suits with it.—Whiles I threat he lives:

Words to the heat of deeds too cold breath gives.
(*A bell rings.*)
I go, and it is done; the bell invites me.
Hear it not, Duncan; for it is a knell
That summons thee to heaven, or to hell.

Now for what I mean. This same idea, these same figures, these same visions, can be better brought before the eye and so into the soul of the audience if the artist concentrates on that which appeals to the eye, than if that which appeals to the brain, and that which appeals to the ear, is making simultaneous confusion.

It is difficult to read this one speech of Macbeth slowly, when other sounds and sights are exterminated and we are quiet in our rooms, and get the full value of what Shakespeare has put there. We can read the speech three, four or five times, and then only is some of its worth caught by us. And having read this speech three, four, five times let anyone continue to read the entire play, and he will be as fatigued as though he had walked twenty miles. But he will have felt some of that which Shakespeare intended him to feel, though by no means all. That which he feels we shall not feel when we go to see the play performed in the theatres.

When we *read* those lines we are not cramped within three walls. We wander up to the top of the castle with Macbeth, we gaze across the rooky woods and across the hills; we can descend with him into the cellars, we may pass out and among

MACBETH

Act V. Scene V.

Macbeth. *To-morrow, and to-morrow, and to-morrow,*
Creeps in this petty pace from day to day,
To the last syllable of recorded time;
And all our yesterdays have lighted fools
The way to dusty death. Out, out, brief candle!
Life's but a walking shadow; a poor player,
That struts and frets his hour upon the stage,
And then is heard no more: it is a tale
Told by an idiot, full of sound and fury,
Signifying nothing.

[*Face page* 118.

the bushes which bank themselves at the foot of the damp castle of Glamis. And if we only went *so* far with Shakespeare I should not have reason to object to the cramping in between three walls which we are subjected to in the theatre; for we should not be great losers. But when we read, we ride with Shakespeare upon the sightless couriers of the air. Pity, like a naked new-born babe, hangs in the air before us; we see the terrifying figure of "wither'd murder" with Tarquin's ravishing strides passing before us; it seems to prowl round the room, the entire time we are reading. We hear the bell which strikes and rings the knell at the death of Duncan. As we sit in our room reading, the bell time after time booms out in the distance. Later, "to-morrow and to-morrow and to-morrow, creeps in this petty pace from day to day." Round our room, outside the window, above us in the room over our head, creeps continually the to-morrow and to-morrow; and so, losing all this in the theatre, we are great losers.

It is not people and things, but ideas which so surround and possess us as we sit and read. And when art is so great and so perfect that it can bring us on the mere reading such priceless magical things, it is little short of sacrilege to destroy that which produces those ideas by confusing us and our other senses by appealing to those other senses at the same time.

How obvious this all should be. And so, although it is absurd to talk hopefully of thc possibility that in a short timc these plays may not be put on the stage, I would have them there but seldom, for the reason I have suggested, that on the stage we lose them.

And there is another reason why I would not have them there, and it is this : the same idea, the same impression—the same beauty and philosophy, if you wish—can be put before the eyes of an audience without at the same time confusing their ideas through an appeal to their other senses.

A man (we may call him Macbeth, though it does not matter what his name is) may be seen passing through all these doubts and fears—a figure in action; and round him other figures in action; and though we may not receive the superb impression which a master (which Shakespeare) gives us, we shall through our eyes receive a clearer impression than if the other senses were called upon at the same time to "assist," for, instead of assisting, they would confuse, as they ever do.

Suppose we look at a picture by Signorelli, the famous one of the Berlin Gallery. I fail utterly to believe that a string quartett playing hard at the same time would assist our eyes; or that some one reciting to us simultaneously the "Birth of Pan" would bring out the qualities in the picture. It would only confuse.

Supposing we are listening to the Pastoral Symphony by Beethoven. I do not believe that a panorama of hay-makers making hay, or a pleasant voice reading to us from Spenser's *Shepheards Calendar* would add in any way to the understanding or the enjoyment of those qualities which are in the Symphony. It would only confuse.

Has it ever been tried? No, indeed! The musicians have protected their garden well. The painters have protected theirs well. The theatre men have left their vineyard, and it has been annexed by any one who wished to make use of it. The playwrights made use of it once: Shakespeare, Molière and the rest. Then Wagner took a fancy to the vineyard. Until to-day we find that the painter is actually making eyes at the little place; the painter, the man who has been given innumerable myriads of acres, a little patch of which he had cultivated till now so exquisitely. But now both painter and musician, as well as the writer, have grown discontented, each with his vast possessions; and so the annexing goes on.

And I am here to tell of this, and I claim the Theatre for those born in the Theatre, and we will have it! To-day, or to-morrow, or in a hundred years, but *we will have it!* So you see I do not wish to remove the plays from the Stage from any affectations, but first because I hold that the plays are spoiled in the theatre, and secondly I hold that the plays and the playwrights are spoiling us, that is to say are robbing us of our self-reliance and our vitality.

In Germany and in England, even in Holland, where they are at times particularly intelligent, they follow up their statement that I wish unreasonably to drive out the plays and the playwrights from the Theatre without reason, by adding *that I wish to introduce the painter in the place of the author.*

What leads them to surmise this is, that I happen to have made very many stage designs on paper. In my time I have produced many pieces on the stage, and in most cases when doing so I have not previously produced designs on paper; and if I possessed a theatre of my own I should not convey on to the paper the designs which are in my mind, but I should place them directly on to the stage.

But as I have not yet this theatre of my own, and as my mind leaves me no rest until these designs and ideas are put into one form or another, I have been forced to make studies of these ideas with the limited means at my disposal. And so I am judged by what is seen on paper and am acclaimed as *Maler* (*painter*); and instantly the thoughtless scream out: "Ha, ha! we have unearthed this terrible conspiracy; this man is only arguing from a little standpoint. He only wants to oust our plays from the stage so that his *pictures* may come there instead."

But, gentlemen, I assure you, you have made

another mistake. A mistake very easy to make and very difficult to avoid making, because you naturally say to yourselves: "If he is not a painter, what is he? He can't be a stage-manager, because a stage-manager first demands a playwright, and this man does not demand a playwright." I see your difficulty perfectly well. How can you understand that which has not been? how can you believe in that which you have not seen? Oh, for a few such men, who, seeing with the mind's eye things which are visionary, believe in the heart of their minds that which they see! Let me repeat again that it is not only the writer whose work is useless in the theatre. It is the musician's work which is useless there, and it is the painter's work which is useless there. All three are utterly useless. Let them keep to their preserves, let them keep to their kingdoms, and let those of the theatre return to theirs. Only when these last are once more re-united there shall spring so great an art, and one so universally beloved, that I prophesy that a new religion will be found contained in it. That religion will preach no more, but it will reveal. It will not show us the definite images which the sculptor and the painter show. It will unveil thought to our eyes, silently—by movements—in visions.

So you see now—I hope you see—that the Theatre has nothing to do with the painter, or painting, just as it has nothing to do with the playwright and literature. You also see that my proposition is a very harmless one—some of you will say a very foolish one—this of restoring our ancient and honourable art. Very harmless, because you see that I am entirely free from antagonism towards the poets or the dramatists; and what feeling I have about the matter is so slight that it will influence the *modern theatre* but little. The modern theatre will retain its place and will go on being the modern theatre until the painter shows a little more fight, and then it will become the more modern theatre, and then some other artist—perhaps the architect—will have his turn; and then the two will fight it out, it will be a beautiful little tussle, and we, the men of the Theatre, that is to say the third dog, will run off with the bone. *Eccola!*

1908.

PEER GYNT

Design for costume.

[*Face page* 124.

THE THEATRE IN RUSSIA, GERMANY AND ENGLAND

TWO LETTERS TO JOHN SEMAR

I

MY DEAR SEMAR,

On leaving Florence you asked me to send you some news of the theatres that I should see in Germany, England and Russia, and I had no sooner arrived at Munich than I wanted to send you news enough to fill three numbers of *The Mask.*

On getting as far as Amsterdam I wanted to send you more news, and now that I am in England I see that it is absolutely necessary to delay no longer.

To write to you about the Art of the Theatre I don't intend, because the Art of the Theatre positively does not exist, but one can write about the activity and inactivity of the Theatre, and if you ask me where the Theatre is most active, I reply it is in Germany. The German activity is not only impulsive but systematic, and this combination is going to bring the German Theatre in twenty years to the foremost position in Europe. I judge by what I see and not by what I hear, and this is what I have seen in Munich.

I have seen princes lending their name and giving

their money to the furtherance of the Theatre. I have seen a new building which has been erected in Munich by the architect, Professor Littmann. I have been over this theatre, and I can assure you that it is first class, that it is not a foolish affair with several balconies one over the other, with unnecessary gilt or marble columns, with unnecessary draperies of plush or silk, or with some vast chandelier, or with the ordinary orchestra boxes and the ordinary stage. It is quite out of the ordinary in every way, and yet you see princes support it, without calling it eccentric, and, what is more, the people support it. I myself tried to obtain a seat for the evening's performance, and although it was at the end of the season, it was impossible to do so. Through the courtesy of Professor Littmann I was able to go on to the stage during the day, and into the auditorium, and I was shown the scenic devices and those for lighting.

They were unlike others that I have seen. The question is not whether they were good or whether they were bad, the only thing that I shall draw your attention to at all is, that although they are entirely new, entirely original, they are receiving support, and not a sort of timid support, but the whole-hearted support of the city of Munich; then I arrive in England to find not one city giving any support from its heart to any original idea which may be in the heads of the younger generation in England, and this is nothing short of disgraceful.

In England we have, I suppose, as much intelligence, as much taste, and perhaps as much genius, as in other lands. Beauty, my dear Semar, the beauty of England is extraordinary, the beauty of its people is amazing, but its energy seems a little bit at rest.

I fully believe that all the artists are playing golf or shooting pheasants. I can imagine that they say to themselves they would rather be in the open air than sitting in a room to be insulted by a lot of rich titled dormice, to whom it has never occurred that there is something better than sleeping. Before I left England, I thought it was the fault of the actor-managers and the men in the theatre. The former seemed to me a most wicked people; but the actor-managers are not entirely to blame. It is the country that is to blame, it is the rich gentlemen of England who are to blame. What right have I for saying this? Why, my stay in Germany of about four years, my visit to Russia and to Holland, and then on the top of it this last stay of two days in Munich. One sees and realizes these things in a flash; one waits, looks, inquires, wonders, and suddenly it becomes quite clear; and unless the gentlemen of England wake up, putting aside the coat of the snob and assuming the coat of the gentleman, the Theatre will not revive—until the day when the English gentleman finds he has lost all his money, that it has been taken by a foreign nation, and in despair he looks round for some one who can help him. Then he will look to the artists and the workers. I am not a Socialist. I love the idea of the swagger lords of England; but it no longer contains swaggering lords with their swaggering ways; they are all somnambulists, white-faced, white-bearded; they creep up and down the towns from Dover to Carlisle, muttering to themselves, " Thank God ! father left me well off. Now I shall have no more worry ! " But they certainly will have a great deal more worry, and it seems to me in a way they don't expect. No ! I am not a Socialist, my dear Semar, not yet !

Now a word or two more about the Munich theatre—the *Münchner Küntsler Theater*, which means the Artist's Theatre of Munich. To a certain section of English artists, perhaps the best section, there is something alarming, something incidentally of what they would call an Art-y theatre, Art with a capital " A." But this Art is not allowed to have a capital " A " as well as any other work ! I have seen War with a capital " W," and what is against Art with a capital " A " ?

I cannot tell you all the plays that they produce, but it is sufficient to speak here of *Faust*, which they commence at six o'clock in the evening in order that they should not be obliged to cut it; of *Das Wundertheater*, the play which possibly many people have not heard of, by that little-known writer, Cervantes; or *Die Deutschen Kleinstädter* or *Twelfth Night* ; besides these, of the *May*

Queen, also of the *Little Dance Legend, Herr Peter Squenz*, and other interesting works.

These productions are the work of the painters and the actors, but they are not unknown actors, nor actors who call themselves independent. They are the actors of the Royal Theatre, that is to say they are what is called conventional actors. I wonder, if there were found a man generous enough to build an Art Theatre in England, whether the chief theatres would lend their actors? The Orchestra in the little Munich theatre is not merely a scratch one, it is the Munich Philharmonic Orchestra!!

Now from such a beginning, from such a combination of actors, musicians and designers (not to speak of the stage-managers, who are the best that can be obtained), much is to be expected. From such a combination in England we could expect as much. Although I was unable to see the performance, I know that it must have been very excellent, and very excellent because very thorough. I did see the stage, and of that I will tell you something.

It was very small, but very complete. Nothing seemed to have been left to chance. Ropes, scenery, lights, seemed to be all out of the way; everything seemed to have been, as it were, put into the cupboard. The scenes which were in use were all hung up, but I cannot describe *how* they were hung up, how well done, how cleverly done. The scene was set for the evening, chairs and tables covered. The scenery, although it had been in use for several months, showed no sign of wear whatever; even the corners where two pieces meet together seemed to be as fresh as the day they were made. Everything seemed so good, so well nursed. I was enchanted by what I saw; it said this one thing to me so clearly: it said, "We Germans are not prepared to say whether the performance will be a work of art or not; we are not prepared to say whether a genius is coming into the theatre or a fool; but we are determined that, whether it be a fool or a genius, he shall find everything in perfect order, and he shall have nothing to complain of as to our arrangements. Unless we give him a good machine (not necessarily an elaborate machine) the work will not have a fair chance."

It would be something to find out the way the Germans set about such a task; it would be very interesting to note whether it is a committee which produces all this system, or whether it is the national training, or whether it is dependent upon a man's personality. I think it must be the national training. "Right-about Turn! Quick March! Eyes Right!" Something of this. The appliances on the stage of the theatre seemed to me to have come from all parts of the earth, for this is the German characteristic, to refuse nothing if he thinks it will be of use.

I have not told you of the building itself. It is beautiful in appearance; it would take too long to describe its charms, but here again its beauty is of secondary importance, what is paramount being its practicalness and its usefulness. You enter the building, and straight in front of you is the box office. On each side are steps leading to your seats, the words indicating the direction you are to take being made part of the decoration, not, as in England, a sort of label on the wall. There is much more to be said, and I will write you again about this and other theatres, and let us hope that soon some united action will be taken in England in this matter of a new theatre. First, that the English gentleman shall understand the part that he is to play; then that the organizer too shall learn what part he is to play; then, finally, that the artist may be called upon to fill the beautiful and systematic theatre with beautiful things.

P.S.—By the by, in going through the stage-door of the theatre I saw there the following words, "Sprechen Streng Verboten," which means "Speaking Strictly Forbidden." The first moment I thought I was in heaven. I thought "At last they have discovered the Art of the Theatre." But no, they have not got so far with the Art. Queer! but the clue is in that very *Sprechen streng verboten*.

ENGLAND, 1908.

II

MY DEAR SEMAR,

I have been intending to write you about the Theatre in England. Perhaps one of these days I may be inspired to fill in a picture post card with the few necessary expressive words, but to-day words fail me to express all I feel about the Theatre in England.

You see I've seen it and the jolly fellows who perpetrate it; they are great fun. I could write you books about them and their genial amiabilities.

I am now in Russia and lodged in the vivid city of Moscow : fêted by the actors of the first theatre here, who are some of the most splendid fellows in the world; and, besides being admirable hosts, they are admirable actors

Soulerzitsky, Moskwin, Artem, Leonidof, Katschalof, Wischnewski, Luschski, Ballif, Adaschef; Frau Lilina, quite delicious; Frau Knipper, magnificent when she wishes; some of the actors in *The Blue Bird* very clever, especially Fraulein Kooneu. Add to these the hundred other actors and actresses who show promise of forming a powerful and united dramatic force; and let me tell you they are one and all intelligent, enthusiastic about their work, working continuously new plays each day, new ideas each minute, and with this to go on you can form for yourself whatever impression you wish.

If such a company could be conjured into existence in England Shakespeare would again become a force. As it is he is merely a stock-in-trade. The Art Theatre here (about which I write) is alive, is possessed of character and intelligence.

Its director, Constantin Stanislawsky, has achieved the impossible : he has successfully established a non-commercial theatre. He believes in realism as a medium through which the actor can reveal the psychology of the dramatist. I don't believe in it. This is not the place to discuss the wisdom or folly of this theory : in the dust jewels are sometimes found; by looking downward the sky can sometimes be seen.

It is quite enough to say that what these Russians do upon their stage they do to perfection. They waste time, money, labour, brains and patience like emperors : like true emperors they do not think they have done all when they have merely spent a lavish sum upon decorations and machinery, although they do not omit to attend to this.

They give hundreds of rehearsals to a play, they change and rechange a scene until it balances to their thought : they rehearse and rehearse and rehearse, inventing detail upon detail with consummate care and patience and always with vivid intelligence—Russian intelligence.

Seriousness, character, these two qualities will guide the Moscow Art Theatre to unending success in Europe or elsewhere. Their theatre was born with a silver spoon in its mouth : it is now only ten years old : it has a long life before it : when it comes of age it will be a firmly established institution. It must take care not to court poetry, and must certainly not wed her, but when it reaches man's estate it will awaken to a new consciousness, spread wings and soar by the two wings of imagination into that vaster and more open path which has no name and leads nowhere beyond itself.

And I am perhaps more miserable than ever before in my life, because I realize the hopeless inactivity of England and its stage, the hopeless vanity and folly of its stage, the utter stupidity of every one connected with the Arts in England, the death-like complaisancy with which London thinks it is active and intelligent about these matters, the idiocy of that section of the Press which calls every courageous attempt to revive life and art "eccentric," that lack of comradeship in London, that lust for *twopence* at all costs. The English actors have no chance; their system of management is bad : they get no chance of study or experience, and dare not rebel or they would lose their bread-and-butter; so they laugh their life away as best they can, that is to say, grimly.

The Russian actors of the Küntslerisches Theater at Moscow give me the impression that they experience a keener intellectual enjoyment during their performances than any other actors in Europe. All their performances are admirable, and whether they touch a play of modern life and modern feeling or a fairy tale, the touch is always sure, always delicate, masterly. Nothing is slipshod. Everything is treated seriously—seriousness, as I have said, is the marked quality of this Russian theatre. Earnestness is never apparent—coming from England this seriousness is possibly more apparent to me than if I were a resident here. In England the spirit of *mockery* is the same force as it was thirty years ago when E. W. Godwin drew attention to the fact. The managers and actors are afraid to be serious, they might be laughed at, they most naturally fear to be merely earnest. In England we find a clever actor laughing at his part and himself, and winking all the time at the audience, horrified least he may be taken seriously. To commit himself would be more than a crime—as Alexandre says, it would be a blunder. Here in Moscow they risk the blunder and achieve the distinction of being the best set of actors upon the European stage. Less of a spontaneous whirlwind than Grasso, their first actor Stanislawsky is more intellectual.

This is not to be misunderstood. You are not to imagine that this actor is cold or stilted. A simpler technique, a more human result, would be difficult to find. A master of psychology, his acting is most realistic, yet he avoids nearly all the brutalities; his performances are all remarkable for their grace. I can find no better word.

I have been most pleased by the performance

of *Onkel Wanja*, although this company is able to handle any play admirably.

In *The Enemy of the People* Stanislawsky shows us how to act Dr. Stockmann without being "theatrical" and without being comic or dull. The audience smile all the time that they are not being moved to tears, but never does a coarse roar go up such as we are used to in the English theatre.

Moscow, 1908.

HAMLET

Act I. Scene IV.

It was this design which I carried over to Germany in 1904, when I first went to Weimar at the invitation of Count Kessler, one of the men who has done most for the German Theatre.

If we had even one such enthusiast of like culture and practical energy in England, the Theatre would be in a more living condition than it is to-day.

This design seems to have given pleasure to my few German friends—and I remember that their pleasure gave me more.

I am not particularly fond of German art, except for its early music, but I am never forgetful of German enthusiasm and of the titanic energy displayed from one end of the land to the other.

And nowhere was there more promise in all Germany than in Weimar in 1904, when Count Kessler lent himself to the task of guiding the taste of the people who were eager to follow him.

In fact, the success of Prof. Reinhardt in Berlin is in a large measure due to the influence and enthusiasm of Count Kessler.

HAMLET

Act I. Scene IV.

It was this design which I carried over to Germany in 1904, when I first went to Weimar at the invitation of Count Kessler, one of the men who has done most for the German Theatre.

If we had even one such enthusiast of like culture and practical energy in England, the Theatre would be in a more living condition than it is to-day.

This design seems to have given pleasure to my few German friends—and I remember that their pleasure gave me more.

I am not particularly fond of German art, except for its early music, but I am never forgetful of German enthusiasms and of the titanic energy displayed from one end of the land to the other.

And nowhere was there more promise in all Germany than in Weimar in 1904, when Count Kessler lent himself to the task of guiding the taste of the people who were eager to follow him.

In fact, the success of Prof. Reinhardt in Berlin is in a large measure due to the influence and enthusiasm of Count Kessler.

[Face page 136.

THE ART OF THE THEATRE THE FIRST DIALOGUE[1]

AN EXPERT AND A PLAYGOER ARE CONVERSING

STAGE-DIRECTOR

YOU have now been over the theatre with me, and have seen its general construction, together with the stage, the machinery for manipulating the scenes, the apparatus for lighting, and the hundred other things, and have also heard what I have had to say of the theatre as a machine; let us rest here in the auditorium, and talk a while of the theatre and of its art. Tell me, do you know what is the Art of the Theatre?

PLAYGOER

To me it seems that Acting is the Art of the Theatre.

STAGE-DIRECTOR

Is a part, then, equal to a whole?

PLAYGOER

No, of course not. Do you, then, mean that the play is the Art of the Theatre?

[1] This Dialogue was published for the first time in 1905. The little book soon went out of print, and for the last three years copies have been unprocurable.

STAGE-DIRECTOR

A play is a work of literature, is it not? Tell me, then, how one art can possibly be another?

PLAYGOER

Well, then, if you tell me that the Art of the Theatre is neither the acting nor the play, then I must come to the conclusion that it is the scenery and the dancing. Yet I cannot think you will tell me this is so.

STAGE-DIRECTOR

No; the Art of the Theatre is neither acting nor the play, it is not scene nor dance, but it consists of all the elements of which these things are composed: action, which is the very spirit of acting; words, which are the body of the play; line and colour, which are the very heart of the scene; rhythm, which is the very essence of dance.

PLAYGOER

Action, words, line, colour, rhythm! And which of these is all-important to the art?

STAGE-DIRECTOR

One is no more important than the other, no more than one colour is more important to a painter than another, or one note more important than another to a musician. In one respect, perhaps, action is the most valuable part. Action bears the same relation to the Art of the Theatre as drawing does to painting, and melody does to music. The Art of the Theatre has sprung from action—movement—dance.

PLAYGOER

I always was led to suppose that it had sprung from speech, and that the poet was the father of the theatre.

STAGE-DIRECTOR

This is the common belief, but consider it for a moment. The poet's imagination finds voice in words, beautifully chosen; he then either recites or sings these words to us, and all is done. That poetry, sung or recited, is for our ears, and, through them, for our imagination. It will not help the matter if the poet shall add gesture to his recitation or to his song; in fact, it will spoil all.

PLAYGOER

Yes, that is clear to me. I quite understand that the addition of gesture to a perfect lyric poem can but produce an inharmonious result. But would you apply the same argument to dramatic poetry?

STAGE-DIRECTOR

Certainly I would. Remember I speak of a dramatic poem, not of a drama. The two things are separate things. A dramatic poem is to be read. A drama is not to be read, but to be seen upon the stage. Therefore gesture is a necessity to a drama, and it is useless to a dramatic poem. It is absurd to talk of these two things, gesture and poetry, as having anything to do with one another. And now, just as you must not confound the dramatic poem with the drama, neither must you confound the dramatic poet with the dramatist. The first writes for the reader, or listener, the second writes for the audience of a theatre. Do you know who was the father of the dramatist ?

PLAYGOER

No, I do not know, but I suppose he was the dramatic poet.

STAGE-DIRECTOR

You are wrong. The father of the dramatist was the dancer. And now tell me from what material the dramatist made his first piece ?

PLAYGOER

I suppose he used words in the same way as the lyric poet.

STAGE-DIRECTOR

Again you are wrong, and that is what every one else supposes who has not learnt the nature of dramatic art. No; the dramatist made his first piece by using action, words, line, colour, and rhythm, and making his appeal to our eyes and ears by a dexterous use of these five factors.

PLAYGOER

And what is the difference between this work of the first dramatists and that of the modern dramatists ?

STAGE-DIRECTOR

The first dramatists were children of the theatre. The modern dramatists are not. The first dramatist understood what the modern dramatist does not yet understand. He knew that when he and his fellows appeared in front of them the audience would be more eager to *see* what he would do than to *hear* what he might *say*. He knew that the eye is more swiftly and powerfully appealed to than any other sense; that it is without question the keenest sense of the body of man. The first thing which he encountered on appearing before them was many pairs of eyes, eager and hungry. Even the men and women sitting so far from him that they would not always be able to hear what he might say, seemed quite close to him by reason of the piercing keenness of their questioning eyes. To these, and all, he spoke either in poetry or prose, but always in action : in poetic action which is dance, or in prose action which is gesture.

PLAYGOER

I am very interested, go on, go on.

STAGE-DIRECTOR

No—rather let us pull up and examine our ground. I have said that the first dramatist was the dancer's son, that is to say, the child of the theatre, not the child of the poet. And I have just said that the modern dramatic poet is the child of the poet, and knows only how to reach the ears of his listeners, nothing else. And yet in spite of this does not the modern audience still go to the theatre as of old to see things, and not to hear things? Indeed, modern audiences insist on looking and having their eyes satisfied in spite of the call from the poet that they shall use their ears only. And now do not misunderstand me. I am not saying or hinting that the poet is a bad writer of plays, or that he has a bad influence upon the theatre. I only wish you to understand that the poet is not of the theatre, has never come from the theatre, and cannot be of the theatre, and that only the dramatist among writers has any birth-claim to the theatre—and that a very slight one. But to continue. My point is this, that the people still flock to *see*, not to hear, plays. But what does that prove? Only that the audiences have not altered. They are there with their thousand pairs of eyes, just the same as of old. And this is all the more extraordinary because the playwrights and the plays have altered. No longer is a play a balance of actions, words, dance, and scene, but it is either all words or all scene. Shakespeare's plays, for instance, are a very different thing to the less modern miracle and mystery plays, which were made entirely for the theatre. *Hamlet* has not the nature of a stage representation. *Hamlet* and the other plays of Shakespeare have so vast and so complete a form when read, that they can but lose heavily when presented to us after having undergone stage treatment. That they were acted in Shakespeare's day proves nothing. I will tell you, on the other hand, what at that period was made for the theatre—the Masques—the Pageants—these were light and beautiful examples of the Art of the Theatre. Had the plays been made to be seen, we should find them incomplete when we read them. Now, no one will say that they find *Hamlet* dull or incomplete when they read it, yet there are many who will feel sorry after witnessing a performance of the play, saying, "No, that is not Shakespeare's *Hamlet*." When no further addition can be made so as to better a work of art, it can be spoken of as "finished"—it is complete. *Hamlet* was finished—was complete—when Shakespeare wrote the last word of his blank verse, and for us to add to it by gesture, scene, costume, or dance, is to hint that it is incomplete and needs these additions.

PLAYGOER

Then do you mean to say *Hamlet* should never be performed?

STAGE-DIRECTOR

To what purpose would it be if I replied "Yes"? *Hamlet* will go on being performed for some time yet, and the duty of the interpreters is to put their best work at its service. But, as I have said, the theatre must not forever rely upon having a play to perform, but must in time perform pieces of its own art.

PLAYGOER

And a piece for the theatre, is that, then, incomplete when printed in a book or recited?

STAGE-DIRECTOR

Yes—and incomplete anywhere except on the boards of a theatre. It must needs be unsatisfying, artless, when read or merely heard, because it is incomplete without its action, its colour, its line and its rhythm in movement and in scene.

PLAYGOER

This interests me, but it dazzles me at the same time.

STAGE-DIRECTOR

Is that, perhaps, because it is a little new? Tell me what it is especially that dazzles you.

PLAYGOER

Well, first of all, the fact that I have never stopped to consider of what the art of the theatre consisted—to many of us it is just an amusement.

STAGE-DIRECTOR

And to you?

PLAYGOER

Oh, to me it has always been a fascination, half amusement and half intellectual exercise. The show has always amused me; the playing of the players has often instructed me.

STAGE-DIRECTOR

In fact, a sort of incomplete satisfaction. That is the natural result of seeing and hearing something imperfect.

PLAYGOER

But I have seen some few plays which seemed to satisfy me.

STAGE-DIRECTOR

If you have been entirely satisfied by something obviously mediocre, may it not be that you were searching for something less than mediocre, and you found that which was just a little better than you expected? Some people go to the theatre, nowadays, expecting to be bored. This is natural, for they have been taught to look for tiresome things. When you tell me you have been satisfied at a modern theatre, you prove that it is not only the art which has degenerated, but that a proportion of the audience has degenerated also. But do not let this depress you. I once knew a man whose life was so occupied, he never heard music other than that of the street organ. It was to him the ideal of what music should be. Still, as you know, there is better music in the world—in fact, barrel-organ music is very bad music; and if you were for once to see an actual piece of theatrical art, you would never again tolerate what is to-day being thrust upon you in place of theatrical art. The reason why you are not given a work of art on the stage is not because the public does not want it, not because there are not excellent craftsmen in the theatre who could prepare it for you, but because the theatre lacks the artist—the artist of the theatre, mind you, not the painter, poet, musician. The many excellent craftsmen whom I have mentioned are, all of them, more or less helpless to change the situation. They are forced to supply what the managers of the theatre demand, but they do so most willingly. The advent of the artist in the theatre world will change all this. He will slowly but surely gather around him these better craftsmen of whom I speak, and together they will give new life to the art of the theatre.

PLAYGOER

But for the others ?

STAGE-DIRECTOR

The others ? The modern theatre is full of these others, these untrained and untalented craftsmen. But I will say one thing for them. I believe they are unconscious of their inability. It is not ignorance on their part, it is innocence. Yet if these same men once realized that they were craftsmen, and would train as such—I do not speak only of the stage-carpenters, electricians, wigmakers, costumiers, scene-painters, and actors (indeed, these are in many ways the best and most willing craftsmen)—I speak chiefly of the stage-director. If the stage-director was to technically train himself for his task of interpreting the plays of the dramatist—in time, and by a gradual development he would again recover the ground lost to the theatre, and finally would restore the Art of the Theatre to its home by means of his own creative genius.

PLAYGOER

Then you place the stage-director before the actors ?

STAGE-DIRECTOR

Yes; the relation of the stage-director to the actor is precisely the same as that of the conductor to his orchestra, or of the publisher to his printer.

PLAYGOER

And you consider that the stage-director is a craftsman and not an artist?

STAGE-DIRECTOR

When he interprets the plays of the dramatist by means of his actors, his scene-painters, and his other craftsmen, then he is a craftsman—a master craftsman; when he will have mastered the uses of actions, words, line, colour, and rhythm, then he may become an artist. Then we shall no longer need the assistance of the playwright—for our art will then be self-reliant.

PLAYGOER

Is your belief in a Renaissance of the art based on your belief in the Renaissance of the stage director?

STAGE-DIRECTOR

Yes, certainly, most certainly. Did you for an instant think that I have a contempt for the stage-director? Rather have I a contempt for any man who fails in the whole duty of the stage-director.

PLAYGOER

What are his duties?

STAGE-DIRECTOR

What is his craft? I will tell you. His work as interpreter of the play of the dramatist is some-

FOR "VENICE PRESERVED"

A Word of Advice to the Beginner.

When some fine day you are asked to Produce *a play, be prepared to produce it* yourself. *If you are prepared you will not only know how to act—but also how to dance—how to draw—how to invent scenes and costumes and "properties." If you are a producer you should be able at least to do all this thoroughly without calling in the assistance of others.*

Some modern "Producers" call in the help of a dancing-master, a designer of costumes and "properties," another designer of scenes . . . they are therefore not practical. They have ideas, like every one else, but as they cannot make those ideas clear to others by practical demonstration, the value of the idea is considerably cheapened as it passes from hand to hand.

The design here is for some "properties" used in "Venice Preserved." It is often supposed that the artist is a vague kind of creature who never goes into detail because he cannot. On the contrary, he must be a man of precision, for his art is founded upon that very quality.

The artist is the man who Does; the amateur is the man who Does not. Make certain that you be an artist of the Theatre, by being able to Do all your own designing, all your own arrangements for dances, fights, limelight effects and acting. For if you call in others to do it for you then you are but a glorious amateur.

FOR "VENICE PRESERVED."

A WORD OF ADVICE TO THE BEGINNER.

When some fine day you are asked to Produce a play, be prepared to produce it yourself. If you are prepared you will not only know how to act—but also how to dance—how to draw—how to invent scenes and costumes and "properties." If you are a producer you should be able at least to do all this thoroughly without calling in the assistance of others.

Some modern "Producers" call in the help of a dancing master, a designer of costumes and "properties," another designer of scenes . . . they are therefore not practical. They have ideas, like every one else, but as they cannot make those ideas clear to others by practical demonstration, the value of the idea is considerably cheapened as it passes from hand to hand.

The design here is for some "properties" used in "Venice Preserved." It is often supposed that the artist is a vague kind of creature who never goes into detail because he cannot. On the contrary, he must be a man of precision, for his art is founded upon that very quality.

The artist is the man who Does; the amateur is the man who Does not. Make certain that you be an artist of the Theatre, by being able to Do all your own designing, all your own arrangements for dances, fights, limelight effects and acting. For if you call in others to do it for you then you are but a glorious amateur.

[*Face page* 148.

thing like this : he takes the copy of the play from the hands of the dramatist and promises faithfully to interpret it as indicated in the text (remember I am speaking only of the very best of stage-directors). He then reads the play, and during the first reading the entire colour, tone, movement, and rhythm that the work must assume comes clearly before him. As for the stage directions, descriptions of the scenes, etc., with which the author may interlard his copy, these are not to be considered by him, for if he is master of his craft he can learn nothing from them.

PLAYGOER

I do not quite understand you. Do you mean that when a playwright has taken the trouble to describe the scene in which his men and women are to move and talk, that the stage-director is to take no notice of such directions—in fact, to disregard them ?

STAGE-DIRECTOR

It makes no difference whether he regards or disregards them. What he must see to is that he makes his action and scene match the verse or the prose, the beauty of it, the sense of it. Whatever picture the dramatist may wish us to know of, he will describe his scene during the progress of the conversation between the characters. Take, for instance, the first scene in *Hamlet*. It begins :—

Ber. Who's there?
Fran. Nay, answer me; stand and unfold yourself.
Ber. Long live the king!
Fran. Bernardo?
Ber. He.
Fran. You come most carefully upon your hour.
Ber. 'Tis now struck twelve; get thee to bed, Francisco.
Fran. For this relief much thanks, 'tis bitter cold,
And I am sick at heart.
Ber. Have you had quiet guard?
Fran. Not a mouse stirring.
Ber. Well, good night.
If you do meet Horatio and Marcellus,
The rivals of my watch, bid them make haste.

That is enough to guide the stage-director. He gathers from it that it is twelve o'clock at night, that it is in the open air, that the guard of some castle is being changed, that it is very cold, very quiet, and very dark. Any additional "stage directions" by the dramatist are trivialities.

PLAYGOER

Then you do not think that an author should write any stage directions whatever, and you seem to consider it an offence on his part if he does so?

STAGE-DIRECTOR

Well, is it not an offence to the men of the theatre?

PLAYGOER

In what way?

STAGE-DIRECTOR

First tell me the greatest offence an actor can give to a dramatist.

PLAYGOER

To play his part badly ?

STAGE-DIRECTOR

No, that may merely prove the actor to be a bad craftsman.

PLAYGOER

Tell me, then.

STAGE-DIRECTOR

The greatest offence an actor can give to a dramatist is to cut out words or lines in his play, or to insert what is known as a "gag." It is an offence to poach on what is the sole property of the playwright. It is not usual to "gag" in Shakespeare, and when it is done it does not go uncensured.

PLAYGOER

But what has this to do with the stage directions of the playwright, and in what way does the playwright offend the theatre when he dictates these stage directions ?

STAGE-DIRECTOR

He offends in that he poaches on their preserves. If to gag or cut the poet's lines is an offence, so is it an offence to tamper with the art of the stage-director.

PLAYGOER

Then is all the stage direction of the world's plays worthless ?

STAGE-DIRECTOR

Not to the reader, but to the stage-director, and to the actor—yes.

PLAYGOER

But Shakespeare——

STAGE-DIRECTOR

Shakespeare seldom directs the stage-manager. Go through *Hamlet*, *Romeo and Juliet*, *King Lear*, *Othello*, any of the masterpieces, and except in some of the historical plays which contain descriptions of possessions, etc., what do you find? How are the scenes described in *Hamlet?*

PLAYGOER

My copy shows a clear description. It has "Act I., scene i. Elsinore. A platform before the Castle."

STAGE-DIRECTOR

You are looking at a late edition with additions by a certain Mr. Malone, but Shakespeare wrote nothing of the kind. His words are "Actus primus. Scæna prima." . . . And now let us look at *Romeo and Juliet*. What does your book say?

PLAYGOER

It says: "Act I., scene i. Verona. A public place."

STAGE-DIRECTOR

And the second scene ?

PLAYGOER

It says : " Scene ii. A street."

STAGE-DIRECTOR

And the third scene ?

PLAYGOER

It says : " Scene iii. A room in Capulet's house."

STAGE-DIRECTOR

And now, would you like to hear what scene directions Shakespeare actually wrote for this play ?

PLAYGOER

Yes.

STAGE-DIRECTOR

He wrote : " Actus primus. Scæna prima." And not another word as to act or scene throughout the whole play. And now for *King Lear*.

PLAYGOER

No, it is enough. I see now. Evidently Shakespeare relied upon the intelligence of the stage-men to complete their scene from his indication. . . But is this the same in regard to the actions ? Does not Shakespeare place some descriptions through *Hamlet*, such as " Hamlet leaps into

Ophelia's grave," "Laertes gràpples with him," and later, "The attendants part them, and they come out of the grave"?

STAGE-DIRECTOR

No, not one word. All the stage directions, from the first to the last, are the tame inventions of sundry editors, Mr. Malone, Mr. Capell, Theobald and others, and they have committed an indiscretion in tampering with the play, for which we, the men of the theatre, have to suffer.

PLAYGOER

How is that?

STAGE-DIRECTOR

Why, supposing any of us reading Shakespeare shall see in our mind's eye some other combination of movements contrary to the "instructions" of these gentlemen, and suppose we represent our ideas on the stage, we are instantly taken to task by some knowing one, who accuses us of altering the directions of Shakespeare—nay more, of altering his very intentions.

PLAYGOER

But do not the "knowing ones," as you call them, know that Shakespeare wrote no stage directions?

STAGE-DIRECTOR

One can only guess that to be the case, to judge from their indiscreet criticisms. Anyhow, what

I wanted to show you was that our greatest modern poet realized that to add stage directions was first of all unnecessary, and secondly, tasteless. We can therefore be sure that Shakespeare at any rate realized what was the work of the theatre craftsman—the stage-manager, and that it was part of the stage-manager's task to invent the scenes in which the play was to be set.

PLAYGOER

Yes, and you were telling me what each part consisted of.

STAGE-DIRECTOR

Quite so. And now that we have disposed of the error that the author's directions are of any use, we can continue to speak of the way the stage-manager sets to work to interpret faithfully the play of the dramatist. I have said that he swears to follow the text faithfully, and that his first work is to read the play through and get the great impression; and in reading, as I have said, begins to see the whole colour, rhythm, action of the thing. He then puts the play aside for some time, and in his mind's eye mixes his palette (to use a painter's expression) with the colours which the impression of the play has called up. Therefore, on sitting down a second time to read through the play, he is surrounded by an atmosphere which he proposes to test. At the end of the second reading he will find that his more definite impressions have received clear and unmistakable corroboration, and that some of his impressions which were less positive have disappeared. He will then make a note of these. It is possible that he will even now commence to suggest, in line and colour, some of the scenes and ideas which are filling his head, but this is more likely to be delayed until he has re-read the play at least a dozen times.

PLAYGOER

But I thought the stage-manager always left that part of the play—the scene designing—to the scene painter ?

STAGE-DIRECTOR

So he does, generally. First blunder of the modern theatre.

PLAYGOER

How is it a blunder ?

STAGE-DIRECTOR

This way : *A* has written a play which *B* promises to interpret faithfully. In so delicate a matter as the interpretation of so elusive a thing as the spirit of a play, which, do you think, will be the surest way to preserve the unity of that spirit ? Will it be best if *B* does all the work by himself ? or will it do to give the work into the hands of *C*, *D*, and *E*, each of whom see or think differently to *B* or *A* ?

PLAYGOER

Of course the former would be best. But is it possible for one man to do the work of three men?

STAGE-DIRECTOR

That is the only way the work can be done, if unity, the one thing vital to a work of art, is to be obtained.

PLAYGOER

So, then, the stage-manager does not call in a scene painter and ask him to design a scene, but he designs one himself?

STAGE-DIRECTOR

Certainly. And remember he does not merely sit down and draw a pretty or historically accurate design, with enough doors and windows in picturesque places, but he first of all chooses certain colours which seem to him to be in harmony with the spirit of the play, rejecting other colours as out of tune. He then weaves into a pattern certain objects—an arch, a fountain, a balcony, a bed—using the chosen object as the centre of his design. Then he adds to this all the objects which are mentioned in the play, and which are necessary to be seen. To these he adds, one by one, each character which appears in the play, and gradually each movement of each character, and each costume. He is as likely as not to make several mistakes in his pattern. If so, he must, as it were, unpick the design, and rectify the blunder even if he has to go right back to the beginning and start the pattern all over again—or he may even have to begin a new pattern. At any rate, slowly, harmoniously, must the whole design develop, so that the eye of the beholder shall be satisfied. While this pattern for the eye is being devised, the designer is being guided as much by the sound of the verse or prose as by the sense or spirit. And shortly all is prepared, and the actual work can be commenced.

PLAYGOER

What actual work? It seems to me that the stage-manager has already been doing a good deal of what may be called actual work.

STAGE-DIRECTOR

Well, perhaps; but the difficulties have but commenced. By the actual work I mean the work which needs skilled labour, such as the actual painting of the huge spaces of canvas for the scenes, and the actual making of the costumes.

PLAYGOER

You are not going to tell me that the stage-manager actually paints his own scenes and cuts his own costumes, and sews them together?

STAGE-DIRECTOR

No, I will not say that he does so in every case and for every play, but he must have done so at one time or another during his apprenticeship, or must have closely studied all the technical points of these complicated crafts. Then will he be able to guide the skilled craftsmen in their different departments. And when the actual making of the scenes and costumes has commenced, the parts are distributed to the different actors, who learn the words before a single rehearsal takes place. (This, as you may guess, is not the custom, but it is what should be seen to by a stage-director such as I describe.) Meantime, the scenes and costumes are almost ready. I will not tell you the amount of interesting but laborious work it entails to prepare the play up to this point. But even when once the scenes are placed upon the stage, and the costumes upon the actors, the difficulty of the work is still great.

PLAYGOER

The stage-director's work is not finished then ?

STAGE-DIRECTOR

Finished ! What do you mean ?

PLAYGOER

Well, I thought now that the scenes and costumes were all seen to, the actors and actresses would do the rest.

STAGE-DIRECTOR

No, the stage-manager's most interesting work is now beginning. His scene is set and his characters are clothed. He has, in short, a kind of dream picture in front of him. He clears the stage of all but the one, two, or more characters who are to commence the play, and he begins the scheme of lighting these figures and the scene.

PLAYGOER

What, is not this branch left to the discretion of the master electrician and his men?

STAGE-DIRECTOR

The doing of it is left to them, but the manner of doing it is the business of the stage-manager. Being, as I have said, a man of some intelligence and training, he has devised a special way of lighting his scene for this play, just as he has devised a special way of painting the scene and costuming the figures. If the word "harmony" held no significance for him, he would of course leave to it the first comer.

PLAYGOER

Then do you actually mean that he has made so close a study of nature that he can direct his electricians how to make it appear as if the sun were shining at such and such an altitude, or as if the moonlight were flooding the interior of the room with such and such an intensity?

STAGE-DIRECTOR

No, I should not like to suggest that, because the reproduction of nature's lights is not what my stage-manager ever attempts. Neither should he attempt such an impossibility. Not to *reproduce* nature, but to *suggest* some of her most beautiful and most living ways—that is what my stage-manager shall attempt. The other thing proclaims an overbearing assumption of omnipotence. A stage-manager may well aim to be an artist, but it ill becomes him to attempt celestial honours. This attitude he can avoid by never trying to imprison or copy nature, for nature will be neither imprisoned nor allow any man to copy her with any success.

PLAYGOER

Then in what way does he set to work ? What guides him in his task of lighting the scene and costumes which we are speaking about ?

STAGE-DIRECTOR

What guides him ? Why, the scene and the costumes, and the verse and the prose, and the sense of the play. All these things, as I told you, have now been brought into harmony, the one with the other—all goes smoothly—what simpler, then, that it should so continue, and that the manager should be the only one to know how to preserve this harmony which he has commenced to create ?

PLAYGOER

Will you tell me some more about the actual way of lighting the scene and the actors ?

STAGE-DIRECTOR

Certainly. What do you want to know ?

PLAYGOER

Well, will you tell me why they put lights all along the floor of the stage—footlights they call them, I believe ?

STAGE-DIRECTOR

Yes, footlights.

PLAYGOER

Well, why are they put on the ground ?

STAGE-DIRECTOR

It is one of the questions which has puzzled all the theatre reform gentlemen, and none have been able to find an answer, for the simple reason that there is no answer. There never was an answer, there never will be an answer. The only thing to do is to remove all the footlights out of all the theatres as quickly as possible and say nothing about it. It is one of those queer things which nobody can explain, and at which children are always surprised. Little Nancy Lake, in 1812, went to Drury Lane Theatre, and her father tells us that she also was astonished at the footlights. Said she :—

> "And there's a row of lamps, my eye !
> How they do blaze—I wonder why
> They keep them on the ground."
>
> —*Rejected Addresses.*

That was in 1812 ! and we are still wondering.

PLAYGOER

A friend of mine—an actor—once told me that if there were no footlights all the faces of the actors would look dirty.

STAGE-DIRECTOR

That was the remark of a man who did not understand that in place of the footlights another method of lighting the faces and figures could be adopted. It is this simple kind of thing which never occurs to those people who will not devote a little time to even a slight study of the other branches of the craft.

PLAYGOER

Do not the actors study the other crafts of the theatre ?

STAGE-DIRECTOR

As a rule—no, and in some ways it is opposed to the very life of an actor. If an actor of intelligence were to devote much time to the study of all the branches of the theatrical art he would gradually cease to act, and would end by becoming a stage-manager—so absorbing is the whole art in comparison with the single craft of acting.

PLAYGOER

My friend the actor also added that if the footlights were removed the audience would not be able to see the expression of his face.

STAGE-DIRECTOR

Had Henry Irving or Elenora Duse said so, the remark would have had some meaning. The ordinary actor's face is either violently expressive or violently inexpressive, that it would be a blessing if the theatres were not only without footlights but without any lights at all. By the way, an excellent theory of the origin of the footlights is advanced by M. Ludovic Celler in *Les Decors, les costumes et la mise en-scéne au XVII. siécle.* The usual way of lighting the stage was by means of large chandeliers, circular or triangular, which were suspended above the heads of the actors and the audience; and M. Celler is of the opinion that the system of footlights owes its origin to the small plain theatres which could not afford to have chandeliers, and therefore placed tallow candles on the floor in front of the stage. I believe this theory to be correct, for common sense could not have dictated such an artistic blunder; whereas the box-office receipts may easily have done so. Remember how little artistic virtue is in the box-office! When we have time I will tell you some things about this same powerful usurper of the theatrical throne—the box-office. But let us return to a more serious and a more interesting topic than this lack of expression and this footlight matter. We had passed in review the different tasks of the stage-manager—scene, costume, lighting—and we had come to the most interesting part, that of the manipulation of the figures in all their movements and speeches. You expressed astonishment that the acting—that is to say, the speaking and actions of the actors—was not left to the actors to arrange for themselves. But consider for an instant the nature of this work. Would you have that which has already grown into a certain unified pattern, suddenly spoiled by the addition of something accidental?

PLAYGOER

How do you mean? I understand what you suggest, but will you not show me more exactly how the actor can spoil the pattern?

STAGE-DIRECTOR

Unconsciously spoil it, mind you! I do not for an instant mean that it is his wish to be out of harmony with his surroundings, but he does so through innocence. Some actors have the right instincts in this matter, and some have none whatever. But even those whose instincts are most keen cannot remain in the pattern, cannot be harmonious, without following the directions of the stage-manager.

PLAYGOER

Then you do not even permit the leading actor and actress to move and act as their instincts and reason dictate ?

STAGE-DIRECTOR

No, rather must they be the very first to follow the direction of the stage-manager, so often do they become the very centre of the pattern—the very heart of the emotional design.

PLAYGOER

And is that understood and appreciated by them ?

STAGE-DIRECTOR

Yes, but only when they realize and appreciate at the same time that the play, and the right and just interpretation of the play, is the all-important thing in the modern theatre. Let me illustrate this point to you. The play to be presented is *Romeo and Juliet.* We have studied the play, prepared scene and costume, lighted both, and now our rehearsals for the actors commence. The first movement of the great crowd of unruly citizens of Verona, fighting, swearing, killing each other, appals us. It horrifies us that in this white little city of roses and song and love there should dwell this amazing and detestable hate which is ready to burst out at the very church doors, or in the middle of the May festival, or under the windows of the house of a newly born girl. Quickly following on this picture, and even while we remember the ugliness which larded both faces of Capulet and Montague, there comes strolling down the road the son of Montague, our Romeo, who is soon to be lover and the loved of his Juliet. Therefore, whoever is chosen to move and speak as Romeo must move and speak as part and parcel of the design—this design which I have already pointed out to you as having a definite form. He must move across our sight in a certain way, passing to a certain point, in a certain light, his head at a certain angle, his eyes, his feet, his whole body in tune with the play, and not (as is often the case) in tune with his own thoughts only, and these out of harmony with the play. For his thoughts (beautiful as they may chance to be) may not match the spirit or the pattern which has been so carefully prepared by the director.

PLAYGOER

Would you have the stage-manager control the movements of whoever might be impersonating the character of Romeo, even if he were a fine actor ?

STAGE-DIRECTOR

Most certainly; and the finer the actor the finer his intelligence and taste, and therefore the more easily controlled. In fact, I am speaking in particular of a theatre wherein all the actors are men of refinement and the manager a man of peculiar accomplishments.

PLAYGOER

But are you not asking these intelligent actors almost to become puppets ?

STAGE-DIRECTOR

A sensitive question ! which one would expect from an actor who felt uncertain about his powers. A puppet is at present only a doll, delightful enough for a puppet show. But for a theatre we need more than a doll. Yet that is the feeling which some actors have about their relationship with the stage-manager. They feel they are having their strings pulled, and resent it, and show they feel hurt—insulted.

PLAYGOER

I can understand that.

STAGE-DIRECTOR

And cannot you also understand that they should be willing to be controlled ? Consider for a moment the relationship of the men on a ship, and you will understand what I consider to be the relationship of men in a theatre. Who are the workers on a ship?

PLAYGOER

A ship? Why, there is the captain, the commander, the first, second and third lieutenants, the navigation officer, and so on, and the crew.

STAGE-DIRECTOR

Well, and what is it that guides the ship?

PLAYGOER

The rudder?

STAGE-DIRECTOR

Yes, and what else?

PLAYGOER

The steersman who holds the wheel of the rudder

STAGE-DIRECTOR

And who else?

PLAYGOER

The man who controls the steersman.

STAGE-DIRECTOR

And who is that?

PLAYGOER

The navigation officer.

STAGE-DIRECTOR

And who controls the navigation officer?

PLAYGOER

The captain.

STAGE-DIRECTOR

And are any orders which do not come from the captain, or by his authority, obeyed ?

PLAYGOER

No, they should not be.

STAGE-DIRECTOR

And can the ship steer its course in safety without the captain ?

PLAYGOER

It is not usual.

STAGE-DIRECTOR

And do the crew obey the captain and his officers?

PLAYGOER

Yes, as a rule.

STAGE-DIRECTOR

Willingly ?

PLAYGOER

Yes.

STAGE-DIRECTOR

And is that not called discipline ?

PLAYGOER

Yes.

STAGE-DIRECTOR

And discipline—what is that the result of ?

PLAYGOER

The proper and willing subjection to rules and principles.

STAGE-DIRECTOR

And the first of those principles is obedience, is it not?

PLAYGOER

It is.

STAGE-DIRECTOR

Very well, then. It will not be difficult for you to understand that a theatre in which so many hundred persons are engaged at work is in many respects like a ship, and demands like management. And it will not be difficult for you to see how the slightest sign of disobedience would be disastrous. Mutiny has been well anticipated in the navy, but not in the theatre. The navy has taken care to define, in clear and unmistakable voice, that the captain of the vessel is the king, and a despotic ruler into the bargain. Mutiny on a ship is dealt with by a court-martial, and is put down by very severe punishment, by imprisonment, or by dismissal from the service.

PLAYGOER

But you are not going to suggest such a possibility for the theatre?

STAGE-DIRECTOR

The theatre, unlike the ship, is not made for

purposes of war, and so for some unaccountable reason discipline is not held to be of such vital importance, whereas it is of as much importance as in any branch of service. But what I wish to show you is that until discipline is understood in a theatre to be willing and reliant obedience to the manager or captain no supreme achievement can be accomplished.

PLAYGOER

But are not the actors, scene-men, and the rest all willing workers ?

STAGE-DIRECTOR

Why, my dear friend, there never were such glorious natured people as these men and women of the theatre. They are enthusiastically willing, but sometimes their judgment is at fault, and they become as willing to be unruly as to be obedient, and as willing to lower the standard as to raise it. As for nailing the flag to the mast—this is seldom dreamed of—for *compromise* and the vicious doctrine of compromise with the enemy is preached by the officers of the theatrical navy. Our enemies are vulgar display, the lower public opinion, and ignorance. To these our " officers " wish us to knuckle under. What the theatre people have not yet quite comprehended is *the value of a high standard and the value of a director who abides by it.*

PLAYGOER

And that director, why should he not be an actor or a scene-painter ?

STAGE-DIRECTOR

Do you pick your leader from the ranks, exalt him to be captain, and then let him handle the guns and the ropes? No; the director of a theatre must be a man apart from any of the crafts. He must be a man who knows but no longer handles the ropes.

PLAYGOER

But I believe it is a fact that many well-known leaders in the theatres have been actors and stage-managers at the same time?

STAGE-DIRECTOR

Yes, that is so. But you will not find it easy to assure me that no mutiny was heard of under their rule. Right away from all this question of positions there is the question of the art, the work. If an actor assumes the management of the stage, and if he is a better actor than his fellows, a natural instinct will lead him to make himself the centre of everything. He will feel that unless he does so the work will appear thin and unsatisfying. He will pay less heed to the play than he will to his own part, and he will, in fact, gradually cease to look upon the work as a whole. And this is not good for the work. This is not the way a work of art is to be produced in the theatre.

PLAYGOER

But might it not be possible to find a great

actor who would be so great an artist that as manager he would never do as you say, but who would always handle himself as actor, just the same as he handles the rest of the material ?

STAGE-DIRECTOR

All things are possible, but, firstly, it is against the nature of an actor to do as you suggest; secondly, it is against the nature of the stage-manager to perform; and thirdly, it is against all nature that a man can be in two places at once. Now, the place of the actor is on the stage, in a certain position, ready by means of his brains to give suggestions of certain emotions, surrounded by certain scenes and people; and it is the place of the stage-manager to be in front of this, that he may view it as a whole. So that you see even if we found our perfect actor who was our perfect stage-manager, he could not be in two places at the same time. Of course we have sometimes seen the conductor of a small orchestra playing the part of the first violin, but not from choice, and not to a satisfactory issue; neither is it the practice in large orchestras.

PLAYGOER

I understand, then, that you would allow no one to rule on the stage except the stage-manager ?

STAGE-DIRECTOR

The nature of the work permits nothing else.

PLAYGOER

Not even the playwright ?

STAGE-DIRECTOR

Only when the playwright has practised and studied the crafts of acting, scene-painting, costume, lighting, and dance, not otherwise. But playwrights, who have not been cradled in the theatre, generally know little of these crafts. Goethe, whose love for the theatre remained ever fresh and beautiful, was in many ways one of the greatest of stage-directors. But, when he linked himself to the Weimar theatre, he forgot to do what the great musician who followed him remembered. Goethe permitted an authority in the theatre higher than himself, that is to say, the owner of the theatre. Wagner was careful to possess himself of his theatre, and become a sort of feudal baron in his castle.

PLAYGOER

Was Goethe's failure as a theatre director due to this fact ?

STAGE-DIRECTOR

Obviously, for had Goethe held the keys of the doors that impudent little poodle would never have got as far as its dressing-room; the leading lady would never have made the theatre and herself immortally ridiculous; and Weimar would have been saved the tradition of having perpetrated the most shocking blunder which ever occurred inside a theatre.

PLAYGOER

The traditions of most theatres certainly do not seem to show that the artist is held in much respect on the stage.

STAGE-DIRECTOR

Well, it would be easy to say a number of hard things about the theatre and its ignorance of art. But one does not hit a thing which is down, unless, perhaps, with the hope that the shock may cause it to leap to its feet again. And our Western theatre is very much down. The East still boasts a theatre. Ours here in the West is on its last legs. But I look for a Renaissance.

PLAYGOER

How will that come ?

STAGE-DIRECTOR

Through the advent of a man who shall contain in him all the qualities which go to make up a master of the theatre, and through the reform of the theatre as an instrument. When that is accomplished, when the theatre has become a masterpiece of mechanism, when it has invented a technique, it will without any effort develop a *creative art* of its own. But the whole question of the development of the craft into a self-reliant

THE VIKINGS

COSTUME DESIGN FOR "SIGURD."

I produced "The Vikings," by Henrik Ibsen, in 1903, for my mother, at the Imperial Theatre, now destroyed. It was what in England is called "an artistic success but a financial failure." Instead of assisting to make the play a success, some of the leading actors did their best to ruin its prospects. Had I been allowed "carte blanche" I should have cleared out the unruly members of the cast, and produced the play a second time—had that failed I should have produced it a third time, probably in a more central theatre, for the "Imperial" certainly was a difficult theatre to find and reach.

If a play is "an artistic success," there is nothing to prevent its financial success. The public, when it knows where it can see a good thing, never fails in time to go and see that good thing. It is a vicious doctrine to teach that the public is a fool. The public is, I take it, the nation, and I am not willing to hear the nation abused by a few middlemen who are not in earnest about anything except making a small living by serving the nation one ill turn after another. The nation should see to it that before long it has better theatre work. For the bad work in the Theatre of to-day has a bad influence on the masses. It is assisting towards the general restlessness which has increased in late years. The public needs masters on whom it can rely—the public is like a woman, but if the so-called "masters" to-day go in so much for what they call humouring the public and giving them nothing, upheavals are bound to ensue.

[Face page 176.

and creative art would take too long to go thoroughly into at present. There are already some theatre men at work on the building of the theatres; some are reforming the acting, some the scenery. And all of this must be of some small value. But the very first thing to be realized is that little or no result can come from the reforming of a single craft of the theatre without at the same time, in the same theatre, reforming all the other crafts. *The whole renaissance of the Art of the Theatre depends upon the extent that this is realized.* The Art of the Theatre, as I have already told you, is divided up into so many crafts: acting, scene, costume, lighting, carpentering, singing, dancing, etc., that it must be realized at the commencement that ENTIRE, not PART reform is needed; and it must be realized that *one* part, one craft, has a *direct* bearing upon each of the other crafts in the theatre, and that no result can come from fitful, uneven reform, but only from a systematic progression. Therefore, the reform of the Art of the Theatre is possible to those men alone who have studied and practised all the crafts of the theatre.

PLAYGOER

That is to say, your ideal stage-manager.

STAGE-DIRECTOR

Yes. You will remember that at the commencement of our conversation I told you my belief in the

Renaissance of the Art of the Theatre was based in my belief in the Renaissance of the stage-director, and that when he had understood the right use of actors, scene, costume, lighting, and dance, and by means of these had mastered the crafts of interpretation, he would then gradually acquire the mastery of action, line, colour, rhythm, and words, this last strength developing out of all the rest. . . . Then I said the Art of the Theatre would have won back its rights, and its work would stand self-reliant as a creative art, and no longer as an interpretative craft.

PLAYGOER

Yes, and at the time I did not quite understand what you meant, and though I can now understand your drift, I do not quite in my mind's eye see the stage without its poet.

STAGE-DIRECTOR

What ? Shall anything be lacking when the poet shall no longer write for the theatre ?

PLAYGOER

The play will be lacking.

STAGE-DIRECTOR

Are you sure of that ?

PLAYGOER

Well, the play will certainly not exist if the poet or playwright is not there to write it.

STAGE-DIRECTOR

There will not be any play in the sense in which you use the word.

PLAYGOER

But you propose to present something to the audience, and I presume before you are able to present them with that something you must have it in your possession.

STAGE-DIRECTOR

Certainly; you could not have made a surer remark. Where you are at fault is to take for granted, as if it were a law for the Medes and Persians, that that *something* must be made of words.

PLAYGOER

Well, what is this something which is not words, but for presentation to the audience ?

STAGE-DIRECTOR

First tell me, is not an idea something ?

PLAYGOER

Yes, but it lacks form.

STAGE-DIRECTOR

Well, but is it not permissible to give an idea whatever form the artist chooses ?

PLAYGOER

Yes.

STAGE-DIRECTOR

And is it an unpardonable crime for the theatrical artist to use some different material to the poet's ?

PLAYGOER

No.

STAGE-DIRECTOR

Then we are permitted to attempt to give form to an idea in whatever material we can find or invent, provided it is not a material which should be put to a better use ?

PLAYGOER

Yes.

STAGE-DIRECTOR

Very good; follow what I have to say for the next few minutes, and then go home and think about it for a while. Since you have granted all I asked you to permit, I am now going to tell you out of what material an artist of the theatre of the future will create his masterpieces. Out of ACTION, SCENE, and VOICE. Is it not very simple ?

And when I say *action*, I mean both gesture and dancing, the prose and poetry of action.

When I say *scene*, I mean all which comes before the eye, such as the lighting, costume, as well as the scenery.

When I say *voice,* I mean the spoken word or the word which is sung, in contradiction to the word which is read, for the word written to be spoken and the word written to be read are two entirely different things.

And now, though I have but repeated what I told you at the beginning of our conversation, I am delighted to see that you no longer look so puzzled.

BERLIN : 1905.

THE ART OF THE THEATRE
THE SECOND DIALOGUE

A PLAYGOER AND A STAGE DIRECTOR SPEAK.

PLAYGOER

I AM glad to see you again after so long an absence. Where have you been ?

STAGE-DIRECTOR

Abroad.

PLAYGOER

What have you been doing all this time ?

STAGE-DIRECTOR

Hunting.

PLAYGOER

Have you turned sportsman, then ?

STAGE-DIRECTOR

I have ; it keeps one in good health. It exercises all the muscles. I shall do better work when I recommence.

PLAYGOER

Tell me about it all, where you have been hunting and what you have bagged.

STAGE-DIRECTOR

I have bagged nothing, for the beast that has occupied me is not caught like a rabbit or a hare, and is far more wary than a fox. Besides, the sport is not in the kill; the sport lies in the difficulties which must be surmounted to get at the beast, and there is no danger at all after you have found him; I have been hunting the monster of a Fable.

PLAYGOER

Which one? The Chimæra, the Hydra or the Hippogriff?

STAGE-DIRECTOR

All of them in one. They are the composite parts of an absurd monster called The Theatrical,[1] and I have tracked this terrible creature into its thousand-and-one caverns and conquered him.

PLAYGOER

You have destroyed him?

STAGE-DIRECTOR

Yes—I have made friends with him.

PLAYGOER

Was there any need for you to have gone abroad to do this simple piece of by-play?

STAGE-DIRECTOR

Certainly, for it was only abroad that I found out the poor thing's weak spots. I was really a little frightened at his roar in England, and the reports of his cave and its collection of dry skulls were certainly most terrifying. But when I got abroad

[1] See note, p. 291.

I began to hunt cautiously, and found him one day dancing, another day making imitations of me, and the third day he invited me into his cave.

Naturally I accepted the invitation and took bearings. I can now bring him down when I will—only the poor dear would never forgive me and I should never forgive myself.

PLAYGOER

I don't know what you are talking about, but I suppose it's all right. It would amuse me much better if you would stay at home and produce a few plays instead of wandering about Europe pretending to hunt.

STAGE-DIRECTOR

But why didn't you say so years ago? I should never have dreamed of foreign lands if you had but signified your desire for me to stay at home. "One must live," as your Dramatic Critic of *The Times* said to the Censor Committee, one cannot merely exist on the spoils of other people's wars; and so I took to sport and have not known a day's disillusion since.

PLAYGOER

And I have never before felt so disillusioned.

STAGE-DIRECTOR

Why, what is the matter with you?

PLAYGOER

I hate the theatre.

STAGE-DIRECTOR

Come now, you exaggerate; you used to love it. I remember you once asked me all sorts of questions about the Art of the Theatre, and we had no end of a talk.

PLAYGOER

I hate it now—I never go inside a theatre now, and the reports, paragraphs, announcements and interviews make me laugh.

STAGE-DIRECTOR

Why is that?

PLAYGOER

That is what I want to know.

STAGE-DIRECTOR

Oh, you want me to be your doctor. You are hungry for the Theatre and you can't swallow it as it is; you want a cure. Well, I can't cure you, for I cannot alter the Theatre in a day or during your lifetime, but if you would like to know what your old love the Theatre is going to be one day I will tell you.

PLAYGOER

You told me that a long time ago, and that has only helped to make me discontented.

STAGE-DIRECTOR

That is what I hoped; but now if you will only be patient I believe I can do something else.

PLAYGOER

Don't tell me anything more about the Art, or the Temples which are to contain the Art, or how its three component parts are Action, Scene and Voice, for all that is more awful to me than your Chimæra Hippogriff monster seemed to you; it is all so enormous, too enormous, and impossible. I must be 6000 years old before it comes, and I must change all my beliefs and customs—so say nothing more about that, I beg of you.

STAGE-DIRECTOR

Agreed. Not a word on that awful subject shall pass my lips—till you permit it.

PLAYGOER

I feel better already. I don't know how it is, but whenever I see you coming an awful dread seizes me; my teeth chatter, my eyes dilate, my hopes leave me. "Will he begin?" I think; "will he start telling me about the Art of the Theatre of the Future?"

You see, it isn't that I don't believe every word you say about it all; what chokes me is to see you taking it all so quietly. I would do much to assist in the realization of your dream, but I see nowhere to begin, and you seem to believe that, when you have told me your idea, it has been realized—you leave no one anything else to do.

STAGE-DIRECTOR

That is not my intention.

PLAYGOER

Maybe not, but that is the impression you leave with me.

STAGE-DIRECTOR

I can only apologize, and now that I have promised not to touch on the *Art* of the Theatre I propose to amuse you with the affairs of the Theatre. To-night you will buy two stalls for a musical comedy.

PLAYGOER

I have not been inside a theatre for two years; that was due to your last talk with me, and now you propose to talk me round again into the Gaiety.

STAGE-DIRECTOR

Yes, that is it. The Gaiety Theatre, two stalls, third row, near the end of the row.

Now to begin—and try and not interrupt me until I have done.

Some years ago I told you about some giant's

work; we talked about the Theatre, and the proportion of my suggestions staggered you. I showed you too much. Since then I have shown more. All this has disheartened you. Now I shall show you less, also the very least. You shall have no complaint to make against me. When I spoke to you before it was as artist, and artists have the same stuff in them as aviators—they can fly. But now I come to earth and shall talk to you like an ordinary stage-manager, who is less of an artist than an administrator; in short, even at the risk of boring a good friend, I shall speak *practically* to you.

You love the Theatre. The fact of your not going inside one for a couple of years proves it. You had a new ideal and you never found it realized there. The ideal to be realized needed artists: there were none in the Theatre. You love the Theatre still; you would give your head for some good reason for going there again, and I am going to give you a reason. It needs you.

PLAYGOER

Maybe: but it no longer interests me. I cannot give my reasons without giving offence to many of those who have formerly given me much pleasure.

STAGE-DIRECTOR

For instance?

PLAYGOER

Well, if I call the actor at the Lyceum theatrical he will be offended; if I find the production at the Elysium vulgar I offend the producer, whom I know personally. Besides, however much I may protest, the actor and the producer are unable to change their methods. I can neither applaud as formerly nor protest as I do to you, and owing to this I am, as I tell you, entirely without interest.

STAGE-DIRECTOR

If the cause of your discontent could be removed your interest would revive?

PLAYGOER

Immediately.

STAGE-DIRECTOR

Tell me, at what are you dissatisfied? I am neither the actor nor the producer.

PLAYGOER

No; but to express it definitely at all would make me feel like a traitor to all I once loved.

STAGE-DIRECTOR

Ah! then it is you that have changed, not the theatres.

PLAYGOER

Perhaps, perhaps.

STAGE-DIRECTOR

And you have developed your sense of what is beautiful. Is it possible, then, that I see before me the ideal spectator in person—that you have become one of that audience which London has been for so long trying to "educate"?

PLAYGOER

No, not that; not so ideal as all that; but maybe you are right that I have developed. The plays and the players cannot have altered so enormously in two years, whereas one's outlook may have changed entirely.

STAGE-DIRECTOR

And now to you everything on the stage looks as "weary, stale, flat and unprofitable" as the world did to Hamlet. But be practical, I beg of you. Look at the matter sensibly. You admit that the stage has not altered, that it is yourself only that has undergone a change. Good! Then undergo another. I do not mean change back again, but change forward.

PLAYGOER

Explain to me what you mean.

STAGE-DIRECTOR

You have looked at the Theatre from two points of view: ascend to a third and better point of view and see what you shall see.

PLAYGOER

That interests me.

STAGE-DIRECTOR

Follow me, then. At present your interest in the Theatre is on a small scale, something like the interest every Englishman takes in his country. You are in the position of a man who dislikes the present government, that is all. The Theatre as an institution is composed of as many parties as are the Houses of Parliament. We have the equivalent of the Conservatives, Liberals, Progressives, Radicals, Socialists, the Labour Party, and even Suffragettes are an established part of our institution.

These parties take themselves all very seriously, and that does no harm. But above and beyond all parties there are the Imperialists—let us call them by this name, at any rate, Idealists. An Imperialist is an Idealist. You once belonged to some theatrical party or other. Let us say you were a Conservative. You thought little about the real Conservatism, but you called yourself a Conservative, and soon you began to weary of the methods of your leaders. You naturally don't wish to be a turncoat, and you are thrown into a state of despondency, not knowing what to do.

PLAYGOER

Well, I can't veer round and become one of the opposite party, can I ?

STAGE-DIRECTOR

Certainly not. You cannot honourably become a member of any other *party*. You cannot court a second disillusion. But there is nothing in the way of your becoming an Imperialist. Bear in mind that I use this word to express the highest ideal, and though I am quite uncertain what the term implies to you; but will you be so good as to accept it (for want of a better) as the best name I can apply to that universal party, or brotherhood, which is composed of people holding or tolerating many different, and opposite, views?

PLAYGOER

Well, then, I am to become an Imperialist. Tell me how to do it.

STAGE-DIRECTOR

My dear fellow, you already look yourself again. You are becoming positively interested. We had better go and look for those seats at the Gaiety at once.

PLAYGOER

No, stay here and go on talking. Tell me how to become an Imperialist.

STAGE-DIRECTOR

Well, you shall book stalls for *Twelfth Night* at His Majesty's Theatre, a bench for the Elizabethan Stage Society's production of *Samson Agonistes*, upper circle for Sir Arthur Pinero's last play at St. James's, and go to the pit at the Court Theatre to see *John Bull's Other Island*. To-night to the Gaiety, to-morrow to hear Bach's Passion Music Drama at St. Paul's, the next evening to the Empire, and in the afternoon to the Cinematograph in Oxford Street. Neither must you omit to go to visit the suburbs to see our great actress as Portia, nor fail to attend one of the British Empire Shakespeare Society's performances. You can do all this in ten evenings, and in the daytime, if you have the time, you could attend one of Mr. Henry Arthur Jones's lectures on the Drama, a meeting of the Actors' Association if you can get an invitation, and a rehearsal of a Drury Lane drama. In short, see the worst and best of everything; see all sides of this work, and I promise you that you will begin to love the Theatre once more.

PLAYGOER

Good-bye. I knew you could not help me. I knew you would tell me to do all this. Why, man, I did all this two years ago!

STAGE-DIRECTOR

You are in a bad state indeed.

PLAYGOER

Yes, but do you not see it is all through you? Some years ago you showed me a visionary picture of what the Theatre might become with its blessed temples and its beautiful art and all the rest of it; and that on the one hand, and this modern Theatre on the other hand, have been to me like deep sea and devil. I can relish neither, so I avoid both.

STAGE-DIRECTOR

Come abroad. I can show you a theatre in the north of Russia that will enchant you.

PLAYGOER

Why do you think so ?

STAGE-DIRECTOR

Because without its being a temple, and all that you seem to dread so in my programme, it is the best ordered theatre in Europe. It is an example of what systematic reform can do in a theatre.

Plays, actors, actresses, managers, scenery, footlights, limelights, opera glasses, realism, all is there, just as in any other theatre, with this difference —that it beats all other theatres at their own game.

There are two kinds of Theatre possible—the natural and the artificial. The European theatres are artificial, and this theatre in the north is also artificial, since it makes use of the same artificial material as that used by the Opera House in Paris or His Majesty's in London. The difference is in the use. Besides this their administration is different from that of other European theatres.

Men are the administrators just the same as in England, and yet the results are different, for the men have remembered something which our administrators have never learned.

PLAYGOER

Stop giving me any more vague notions of this theatre and tell me in detail something of its method.

STAGE-DIRECTOR

With pleasure. This theatre is better than others both in the work of the stage and in the manner of the administration.

PLAYGOER

In what does the work of the stage differ ? You say they do not use different material from that employed by the other theatres ?

STAGE-DIRECTOR

No, the same. They use actors who paint their faces, scenes painted on canvas and stretched upon wood, footlights and other artificial lights, blank verse, phonographs and all the rest of it; but they make use of these things with taste.

PLAYGOER

But do none of the other European theatres do this ?

STAGE-DIRECTOR

Other European theatres make only a casual study of this strange artificial material, and so they are unable to express with any distinction, and the canvas and the paint appear as mere canvas and paint, things which in themselves are not interesting.

PLAYGOER

Then is there no other theatre where they use these things with taste?

STAGE-DIRECTOR

No.

PLAYGOER

I suppose the workers in the Russian theatre are able to use their material more tastefully because they have more technical knowledge?

STAGE-DIRECTOR

Yes, though I don't understand why you ask so obvious a question. What do you mean? If instead of a casual study they give serious and *thorough* study to their material it stands to reason that their technique is more perfect.

PLAYGOER

But consider the performances at the leading London theatres, for example. Is there no technique shown in the use of these materials there?

STAGE-DIRECTOR

If this were so I should not have said no. But I will give you an instance of what I mean. Take, for example, the matter of scenic mechanism.

There are at least nine or ten professional ways of bringing a moon on to the stage. We know how the company of actors of Messrs. Bottom and Quince introduced their moon; we know how the sumptuous revival gentlemen manage it in England; we know how the opera manages it, and we know how Professor Herkomer manages it. All these ways differ in so far as one inventor has been more careless than another in studying the exact way in which the moon performs its part.

Now, after the ten different ways have been carefully studied by the workers in the Constan Theatre they will find six other ways, will reject five of them and adopt the sixth, which will be the best. And this sixth way will far exceed all other ways seen in Europe. I mean, of course, technically, for naturally art has nothing to do with the reproduction of moons on the stage, and art is not what we are talking about here. But in every other way this moon will be more like actuality than any other moon which the theatre of Europe has seen for centuries.

PLAYGOER

How can you make such a statement? You are not even half a century old.

STAGE-DIRECTOR

No; but when a good idea has been found in the theatre, especially a good idea for reproducing some effect in Nature, it is never forgotten. Those are the things by which the greatest store is laid. Remember, I am not holding a brief for the Constan Theatre in any way except in the production of plays in which they desire to bring realistic effects, and I state that for the first time realistic effects are actually produced, that there is no slipshod work and no avoiding the difficulty by doing what "was done last time."

PLAYGOER

You have only proved, however, that they have more independence and are freer in rejecting traditional tricks; you have not proved to me that what they do is in better taste.

STAGE-DIRECTOR

Well, I can but tell you it is more like Nature. Would you say that to be like Nature is in better taste, or would you say that to be like the Theatre is in better taste?

PLAYGOER

Certainly to be like Nature.

STAGE-DIRECTOR

Very well, then, your question is answered.

PLAYGOER

But how do the workers in this theatre arrive at this technical perfection which enables them to use their material with such taste?

STAGE-DIRECTOR

How do you arrive at a technical knowledge of anything ?

PLAYGOER

By study, of course; but are these the only theatrical workers in all Europe who do study ?

STAGE-DIRECTOR

I think we are speaking of technical *perfection?* Well, then, you did not ask me whether they had a superficial knowledge of their craft. There are plenty of people who study, but who study badly. The Constan people study and experiment more carefully.

PLAYGOER

And perhaps they have more talent ?

STAGE-DIRECTOR

Possibly. And, as you know, talent is a thing which develops by study.

PLAYGOER

Have they anything at Constan in the nature of a school in which to study ?

STAGE-DIRECTOR

Yes, their theatre is a school. They are in the theatre from morning till night all the year round, save for a few weeks' holiday in the summer. In England you can go into a theatre on many days in the year and find no one there except the carpenters and the stage-director and a few other officials. In Constan the place is crowded all day and night, and if there is a rehearsal the students are there to witness it; and not giggling and playing the fool, but watching every movement and listening to every word.

PLAYGOER

Whom do you mean by the students?

STAGE-DIRECTOR

Everybody. They are all students. There are the two directors to begin with (the third director occupies himself only with affairs); and these two directors are as much students as any one else: they are studying all the time. Then come the leading actors and actresses. There are about twelve of these, each one as good as any star in Europe. But what am I saying? Each one is a much better actor or actress than the greatest stars in Europe. Then there are about twenty-four actors and actresses of what are called "secondary parts." Many of these are brilliant enough to be included in the first category, only they have not served their apprenticeship long enough.

PLAYGOER

What? If an actor shows especial talent is he not moved up to the first rank at once?

STAGE-DIRECTOR

No, certainly not. Not until he has gone

through the same experience as the others, no matter how talented he may be. Then, besides these whom I have named, there are the very young students. There are about twenty of these. They are most of them men and women from the universities; and the girls are not chosen just because they look pretty, but, with the men, are selected for their capabilities.

PLAYGOER

Is this not so in other lands?

STAGE-DIRECTOR

Most certainly not. Half the girls on the English stage are chosen because they look pretty.

PLAYGOER

But an actress's looks are surely a matter of importance?

STAGE-DIRECTOR

Yes, of great importance, and should form part of her studies. It has never occurred to the English actresses that it is a part of their work, and a part which needs great talent and application, to make themselves look nice. Some of your most talented actresses in England are by no means what are called pretty girls. That is to say, their features are far from perfect, their complexions are not so fresh as that of an Irish girl on the lakes, but they have the talent by which they can make themselves look this, or that, or the other. Just as it is a part of the actor's talent and study to be able to make his face into a grotesque mask, so is it part of an actress's talent and study to make herself look beautiful when she wishes. When this is fully realized young ladies will cease putting their looks forward as a reason for obtaining an engagement, and the stage will be less overcrowded and better filled.

But now, to return to the number of workers at Constan. We had got as far as the students. Besides and below these are the probationers.

PLAYGOER

Who are they ?

STAGE-DIRECTOR

They are young people who apply to be admitted to the theatre as students. They are told that they must work for a certain time—I believe one or two years—in order to become candidates for the school. Then after an examination before the directors and stage-managers and actors some of them are selected and put into the school.

PLAYGOER

What kind of examination do they undergo ?

STAGE-DIRECTOR

Each candidate prepares a poem and a fable for recitation. And the examination of the candidates at this theatre proves conclusively that it is the directors of the theatre, and not the Russians, that are so remarkable; for these candidates are no different from any other stage aspirants in regard to their talent for dramatic expression. They are different from other students only in that they are more educated than other theatrical aspirants, many of them having a considerable knowledge of literature, foreign languages, art and science.

On passing their examination they are put into the school, in which they work daily for a term of years, and in the evenings they may be required to fill those parts known as "walking on parts." Thus, while they are studying at the school they are in the midst of the acting nearly every evening, and at the end of a few years it is possible, or nearly certain, that they may be offered a small engagement by the theatre in which they are working. So that here we have, you see, a standing company of about one hundred.

PLAYGOER

What do you mean by a standing company ?

STAGE-DIRECTOR

The same as is meant by a standing army.

PLAYGOER

Then do not the actors leave to take better engagements ?

STAGE-DIRECTOR

No, for there can be no better engagement. To be a member of the Constan Art Theatre is the ambition of every actor in Russia.

PLAYGOER

Would a very talented actor from another theatre apply for membership in this company ?

STAGE-DIRECTOR

Maybe; but it would take him some time to get into the particular atmosphere which has been created by this company, and in order to do this he would possibly have to take very small parts to begin with.

PLAYGOER

Then the work there differs entirely from that in other theatres, and any one entering would feel very much at sea ?

STAGE-DIRECTOR

Precisely.

PLAYGOER

Are all the students training to be actors ?

STAGE-DIRECTOR

Yes.

PLAYGOER

Then, they do not train stage-directors ?

STAGE-DIRECTOR

Before you can be a stage-director you must have

first been an actor. Their stage-directors are only produced last of all. After they have been several years acting it may be that one or another will show some talent as stage-manager. This talent is given an opportunity for showing itself and developing itself in the following manner—

At the end of each season the school performs certain scenes from about ten or twelve different plays. In 1909, among the plays which the students selected were the following: *Elga* and *Hannele* by Hauptmann, a play by Sudermann, *When We Dead Awaken* by Ibsen, *La Locandiera* by Goldoni, *La Citta Morta* by D'Annunzio, *L'Avare* by Molière, and about three or four plays by Russian authors.

These scenes are in each case represented by different members of the school, and a different stage-manager is selected for each. The performance takes place in the afternoon. The relations of the students are invited, the directors of the theatre, together with the company, are also present, and the performance affords an opportunity of revealing any talent for stage-management or for acting which may be latent in the students. The talent displayed in 1909 was, in my opinion, nothing short of remarkable. Each stage-manager has at his disposal all that the theatre has to offer him, though of course it is impossible to paint new scenes; still, he can show his talent by the use of what is at hand.

PLAYGOER

You spoke to me once long ago about an ideal stage-manager, a man who would combine all the talents, who had been actor, scene and costume designer; who understood the lighting of the play, the formation of dance, and the sense of rhythms; who could rehearse the actors in their parts; who could, in short, with his own brain, finish that work which the poet, for all stage purposes, had left in an unfinished condition. Do you find any such in Constan ?

STAGE-DIRECTOR

I find the nearest approach to such a man. There is very little that the *régisseurs* there cannot do.

PLAYGOER

There are many people who would say that after all there is nothing very different in this theatre from other theatres except the difference of its greater thoroughness.

STAGE-DIRECTOR

Then, now, I will try and show you wherein the essential difference really lies. I have been able so far to explain to you something of the system. I have tried to show you how superior the Russian method is to any other, but I still do not expect you to understand entirely what I mean, and I admit that it would be utterly impossible to explain the chief reason of this theatre's superiority till you have come into touch with the men who have trained in the theatre and, above all, with the man who has trained them—the director. There lies the secret, and it will be buried with him. You would understand what I have been telling you if you were to see him, but even then you still could not lay his secret bare to any practical advantage.

PLAYGOER

Do you who have seen him understand their secret?

STAGE-DIRECTOR

I understand it; but I could not make any one else understand it, for the reason that it is one of those simple things which no amount of coaxing can create, and no amount of antagonism can destroy, and no amount of explanation explain.

PLAYGOER

And what is it?

STAGE-DIRECTOR

Passionate love for the Theatre; and I can say to you without any fear of being thought profane: "Greater love hath no man than this, that a man lay down his life for his work."

PLAYGOER

But do they not love the stage in this way in the other theatres?

STAGE-DIRECTOR

No, they do not—they do not. There are other things for which they would far sooner give their lives before their work; for social success, financial success. They are only willing to devote their lives if they can get either of these things in exchange. In Constan they have but one desire—that is, to do the best work. Do you think I am severe upon the other theatres ?

I am not. I am prepared to tell any theatre what it is working for and to point out the difference between its aim and that of the Constan Theatre. I call to mind the best theatres in Europe and I see clearly what it is they want. It is quite possible that there are many theatres unknown to me, and that in those theatres there are men to whom I do a great injustice by seeming to include them in this accusation; but I speak only of those theatres known to me. They are supposed to be the first theatres in Europe. In my opinion they are the very last. Yet it would be quite possible for the other theatres to be as good as the Constan Art Theatre, that is to say, in the first line, by merely being possessed of the same *passionate love for the Theatre.*

And now to tell you a few things about the Administration.

PLAYGOER

That is what I want to hear about.

STAGE-DIRECTOR

To begin with, the administration is in the hands of a board of directors. There is the president, five members of the board, and the secretary, and five out of these seven are artists. The capital is vested in a stock company composed of merchants of the city of Constan, and, like other stock companies, the money and affairs are administered by a board of directors.

PLAYGOER

Then so far it does not differ from other theatres ?

STAGE-DIRECTOR

No ? Is it usual then for artists to be in the majority on the board of directors ? I think you have overlooked this. But now tell me something. I am a man entirely innocent of business. Supposing I had found people to have enough faith in me to put down fifty thousand pounds to establish an Art Theatre in England what would be the feeling exhibited on the last day of the year when the report was read out to the shareholders showing that there was not a penny of dividend ?

PLAYGOER

The shareholders would examine the books, and, having found that the expenses exceeded the income, they would probably change the management, and advise the production of more popular pieces, which would bring more money into the box office.

STAGE-DIRECTOR

Why would they do this ?

PLAYGOER

Because they put their money into the theatre with the idea of making more by it.

STAGE-DIRECTOR

Suppose you were yourself a shareholder, and I were to point out to you that this thing could not possibly pay for one, two, or even three years, what would you say, knowing that there had been a deficit on the first year ?

PLAYGOER

I should want to examine the situation very thoroughly.

STAGE-DIRECTOR

Oh, then, you would not entirely back out of it ?

PLAYGOER

I should look into the matter thoroughly first.

STAGE-DIRECTOR

I should take it, then, that you had become a shareholder because you were interested not only in the making of money but in the work itself ?

PLAYGOER

Yes; but as I am a business man my primary object would be to make money.

STAGE-DIRECTOR

Would you think that it would be a practical move on your part to go on supporting such a theatre if it paid no dividend for the first three, four, or five years ?

PLAYGOER

No, I should not.

STAGE-DIRECTOR

Well, then, explain to me as a business man how it is that there have been business men found in the town of Constan *who are content to wait for ten years to see the first return for their money ?*

PLAYGOER

It is inexplicable to me. But I suppose that the making of money must to them have been a secondary consideration to the furthering of art. And really, if I were an extremely wealthy man myself I should look on that as a luxury or a hobby, and one which I could take pride in being connected with.

STAGE-DIRECTOR

Well, you told me you were losing your interest in the drama, and you are a wealthy man. Here is a way to revive your interest. Connect yourself with such a theatre. You will remember that I told you a little time ago that the Theatre needed you. I now see the more clearly that you are the very man it needs. But first of all let us see whether, should you take such a charming step, you might not gain in every way without losing your money. Let us return to the theatre at Constan and see what happened there.

PLAYGOER

Yes. But tell me one thing. When was the first dividend declared ?

STAGE-DIRECTOR

At the end of ten years.

PLAYGOER

But that might happen in any theatre; it sounds bad business, but is not peculiar to any particular enterprise.

STAGE-DIRECTOR

Yes; but the fact that after ten years we find the original list of shareholders unchanged, and not only unchanged but increased, is rather unusual, is it not ? and certainly most encouraging. Do you not find it so ?

PLAYGOER

Yes, both encouraging and inspiring. I really do think that what you tell me is quite splendid. But could it be done anywhere else ?

STAGE-DIRECTOR

Have you any good reason for thinking that it could not be done ?

PLAYGOER

The fact that like propositions have failed in England.

STAGE-DIRECTOR

Has the test ever been made ?

PLAYGOER

Probably not, for I doubt if anybody of such men as you describe as forming the Constan stock company could be found in England.

STAGE-DIRECTOR

Then hath not an Englishman eyes, hath not an Englishman hands, organs, dimensions, senses, passions, affections ? Surely you must be wrong in what you say ?

PLAYGOER

I think not; because the drama in England and also in America has become merely another commercial means for the making of money.

STAGE-DIRECTOR

So it is all over Russia—all over Europe. But if you can find thirty or forty such men in Russia you can surely find thirty or forty in England. Besides, think, what is the New Theatre in New York but such a theatre ? Do you think that its founders want to see a return for their money in the first two years ?

PLAYGOER

They might wait for two or three years before

receiving a dividend, but they are not likely to wait for ten; although I do not think that the making of money is their primary object.

STAGE-DIRECTOR

Well, then, why do you think these millionaires have put their money into this theatre ?

PLAYGOER

Because I think they have been brought to a realization that something has got to be done for the drama in America, and being men in a leading position they feel they are expected to do it.

STAGE-DIRECTOR

And if at the end of, let us say, five years, the public agrees that the work being done in the theatre is perfect, yet the directors know that there has been no profit, will they continue to support it, or will they say that the work is less perfect because the theatre has failed to return a dividend ?

PLAYGOER

If they realized that the public was satisfied they would continue. But tell me, if the public was satisfied would not that mean that the theatre had been full every evening ?

STAGE-DIRECTOR

Not exactly, though it might mean that it had been very fairly full every evening. But you must not forget that the expenses of running such a theatre are very great. The Constan Art Theatre, for instance, had very nearly full houses for nearly ten years, but its expenses exceeded its income.

PLAYGOER

Do you not call that bad business ?

STAGE-DIRECTOR

I cannot give an opinion upon business. But let me put it to you more clearly, and do you then decide. This Russian theatre has had full houses, it has produced plays which the public has said are perfect; it is the first theatre in the land; it has done what it set out to do. Do you not call that good business ?

PLAYGOER

Yes, I do.

STAGE-DIRECTOR

Would you call it good business to have built up a reputation which is second to none in Europe ? —to be able to command a vast public and the enthusiastic support of staunch shareholders ?

PLAYGOER

Yes, I suppose I should.

STAGE-DIRECTOR

You would agree that the shareholders have in their possession something by means of which they can now realize what money they like ?

PLAYGOER

How can they do so ?

STAGE-DIRECTOR

By building a second theatre, a large theatre, and by touring round the world.

PLAYGOER

Where is the money coming from when you say that they have only just begun to realize a slight dividend ?

STAGE-DIRECTOR

It will be found. When you ask me to say how, why I can only refer you to the work of the last ten years. Nothing daunted the workers in this theatre, or seemed to deter them from doing what they wanted to do. They will build this theatre, they will continue to give the public the best works in the best way, and they will set an example to the rest of Europe.

PLAYGOER

Rather a costly example !

STAGE-DIRECTOR

Not so costly when you think of it for a moment. It is the belief in Europe that the Russians are composed of people less interested in art than any one else. In this their reputation resembles that of the English. There is a general idea also that they are a kind of savage race, and by making this demonstration through the artistic theatre they have shown clearly that they are nothing of the kind. In a way this is really a national theatre in the best sense of the word, for the shareholders have the interests of their nation at heart. This theatre, as I have said, will no doubt visit the centres of Europe, and at each visit the refincment and culture and courage of Russia will be made manifest. In short, it is a very clever commercial stroke on a very large scale, and English men could do worse than follow their lead. Money that has been sunk in this theatre is not wasted money, and we shall shortly see the fruits of it. Don't you think that is so?

PLAYGOER

Yes, I think so; but looking at it in that light, it takes it right away from the commercial theatre.

STAGE-DIRECTOR

Why, of course it does. I was speaking of the theatre as an asset of the nation.

PLAYGOER

Yes? Well, we are going to have a National Theatre in England.

STAGE-DIRECTOR

Not at all. We are going to have a Society Theatre. That in my opinion is very much what the New Theatre in America is—a society theatre. Now nobody wants a society theatre, least of all the ladies and gentlemen who are obliged to go and sit in their boxes and stalls while they are bored to death by the dull performances which take place on the stage. Such society theatres bore and impoverish every city of Europe. There is the Opéra in Paris, the Schauspielhaus in Berlin, in Munich, in Vienna. They are not national Theatres in the real sense of the word. The men who will make a national theatre in England are the same kind of men as those who have made this theatre in Russia. If they are to be expensive they must not be a bore, these theatres. The proposed "national" theatre for London is national in name only. It has no programme, and yet it asks for subscriptions on the strength of one. The committee may force subscriptions, but no amount of forcing can raise the wits—and it is wits and taste that we want in our Theatre. Now the Russians commence founding their national theatre by first founding an artistic theatre and testing its honesty of purpose for ten years. Which of these strikes you as the better method of obtaining a finely organized national theatre—the English or the Russian? Which is the most economic, the most regular? Which seems to you the *rightest?* In short, if you had a theatre which method would you yourself employ?

PLAYGOER

The Russian method—if I had the type of men and the same point of view.

STAGE-DIRECTOR

Their point of view differs very slightly from that of any of the English managements, for we must believe the English managers when they assure us that their aim is to do the best possible work. Perhaps the men are of a different strain. But you could find as clever and as enthusiastic fellows over here, and if there is less sympathetic understanding of each other's wishes there is more sense of discipline in Englishmen.

PLAYGOER

Then a theatre such as the Constan Art Theatre could be founded here ?

STAGE-DIRECTOR

A theatre, yes; and two or three such theatres.

PLAYGOER

That would indeed be an excellent thing.

STAGE-DIRECTOR

And is it not practical ?

PLAYGOER

I should say absolutely practical.

STAGE-DIRECTOR

Ah, how quick you are to see it and to acquiesce now that it has been DONE ! If I were to say that what I had been telling you was but an idea of mine, which I believed in entirely, would that convince you as to its practicality ? You are one of the dearest good fellows, but, by Jove, when you are asked to believe in that which does not yet exist you are as coy about the whole thing as though you were a woman.

The Constan Art Theatre has been in existence for over ten years, so you believe in it and cry out that it is "absolutely practical."

PLAYGOER

Well, but isn't it ? And how can you ask any one in his senses to believe in a scheme which has not been tried ?

STAGE-DIRECTOR

Caution is never bad : it is the English habit of being over-cautious that blights so many, many spirited ideas which only need the right support to bring them into the plane of actuality. And it is not only in withholding monetary support that Englishmen are over-cautious : it is their moral support which is so often absent, which implies that in such matters they are sometimes very much lacking in moral courage.

And now tell me again. Do you find the Russian method perfectly practical ?

PLAYGOER

Yes, I think it is perfectly practical.

STAGE-DIRECTOR

And if I should say that though it is a very practical method of carrying on a modern theatre, which has to open its doors to the public night after night, there is even a more practical method of pursuing the study of the Art of the Theatre, what would you say ?

PLAYGOER

I should say—— But explain more fully what you mean.

STAGE-DIRECTOR

I mean this : the object of all Ideal Theatres—and their directors—is to excel in the art which it is their privilege to serve. They must be unceasing in the pursuit of the ideal, they must ever aim to go beyond, and therefore they must be very, very far-sighted. Am I right ?

PLAYGOER

I suppose you are. Are the directors at Constan not far-sighted ?

STAGE-DIRECTOR

Very far-sighted where their theatre is concerned, less so where the art is concerned. They have to keep their theatre open night after night; it is one of the difficulties with which they are always contending. If they could close their theatre for five years and spend that time in making nothing but experiments they would have more time for the pursuit of the Ideal, which we have put down as being the object of all ideal theatres.

PLAYGOER

To close such a theatre for five years would be a very serious step to take.

STAGE-DIRECTOR

Very serious; just so serious as the occasion demands. Most theatres in Europe might be closed indefinitely all the year round for fifty years and make experiments all the time without any valuable results, but this theatre in Constan is the exception, and it might just discover the heart of the mystery by so doing. And I think we should be just so far-sighted as to see how serious is the present position of the Theatre.

PLAYGOER

But no one can see farther than the vanishing point at any time, and I presume that point to be the limit which you set to the sight of any director —it is the farthest he can see.

STAGE-DIRECTOR

Perfectly correct; but remember with each advancing step the position of the vanishing point alters, and we are thus enabled continually to see farther than before.

PLAYGOER

That is true.

STAGE-DIRECTOR

Therefore an art director of a theatre who strives to surpass his last achievement will keep his eyes fixed upon this vanishing point on the horizon, and will thereby be enabled continually to achieve his ever-fixed but ever-changing desire to advance, no matter how slowly he may do so. Do you agree with me?

PLAYGOER

I do.

STAGE-DIRECTOR

What, then, is practical to him?

PLAYGOER

All that lies before him and all that he can see.

STAGE-DIRECTOR

And if he advance five steps he will see less than should he advance a hundred steps?

PLAYGOER

Yes, certainly—twenty times less.

STAGE-DIRECTOR

And if he advance five hundred steps he will see a hundred times more than if he advance but five steps?

PLAYGOER

Yes; there is no doubt about it.

STAGE-DIRECTOR

And he will therefore be able to achieve a hundred degrees more than by advancing five steps and seeing five degrees farther?

PLAYGOER

That is true.

STAGE-DIRECTOR

Then, practically speaking, there is no limit to his achievements provided he can only see far enough ahead; and in order to see very far he must have advanced almost as far as he can see. They say that art is long and life is short. Do you believe, then, that there is much time to spare in delays, or would you advise those who are searching forwards to advance without hesitation?

PLAYGOER

The latter, but with caution.

STAGE-DIRECTOR

Yes, with caution and deliberation; but you will remember that we proved that it was entirely safe for a man to advance provided he went towards that which was visible to him. Now we must see which is the best method of reaching a spot which is visible to us. Do you think it is by going backwards?

ROMEO AND JULIET

Act I. Scene V.

This design depends much on its colour to express the exact feeling I wished to convey. So think of it as bathed in a warm yellow light—the only other colour being the touches of green in the dresses of the Italian gentlemen who are awaiting the arrival of their guests. The large seat is silvery white—upon this the two lovers are soon to find themselves seated side by side.

[*Face page* 224.

PLAYGOER

Certainly not. How could it be?

STAGE-DIRECTOR

Or by going sideways, perhaps?

PLAYGOER

No, of course not.

STAGE-DIRECTOR

Or moving in a circle, for caution's sake?

PLAYGOER

No. None of these ways would serve.

STAGE-DIRECTOR

Why not?

PLAYGOER

Why, they would be absurd. When you have seen something the best way to reach it is to go straight towards it.

STAGE-DIRECTOR

Has this method ever been put into practice with success?

PLAYGOER

Yes; nearly always.

STAGE-DIRECTOR

In a hundred cases how often would you say it has been successful?

PLAYGOER

I should say in ninety cases out of a hundred.

STAGE-DIRECTOR

I should think you are right, and should myself be inclined to say that a man can reach that which he can see in ninety-nine cases out of a hundred by going straight towards the object. The hundredth time I waive the right as acknowledgment to the Goddess Fortuna. It is also reasonable to suppose that by doing so he will, as we have said, save much time.

PLAYGOER

That is also true; but may I beg you to tell me what this has to do with the Theatre?

STAGE-DIRECTOR

I must ask you to follow me back to that point, the Theatre, a point which you have perceived, in a straight line and without any delay. Will you tell me whether the eyes are generally used for seeing with?

PLAYGOER

Why, yes; of course they are.

STAGE-DIRECTOR

And would you say that, in order to see, it is more practical to open the eyes than to close them?

PLAYGOER

The former seems to be more sensible.

STAGE-DIRECTOR

You do not answer my question. Is it also practical ?

PLAYGOER

It is.

STAGE-DIRECTOR

And would you say that to look in the direction where you have seen something a while ago is to stand a good chance of seeing it again ? Would you say that it is practical ?

PLAYGOER

I should.

STAGE-DIRECTOR

And on arriving at the spot seen, and seeing farther on a second spot, would it be practical to advance farther in the same direction, so as to reach it ?

PLAYGOER

It would.

STAGE-DIRECTOR

Very well, then ; you have told me what I always suspected to be the truth. You have said that an artist with imagination is justified, and entirely practical, in advancing towards that which he has once seen in his imagination. Therefore, my dear fellow, you have only now to tell me one thing more.

PLAYGOER

What is that ?

STAGE-DIRECTOR

You must tell me whether it is possible for all people to see the same thing.

PLAYGOER

It is very unlikely.

STAGE-DIRECTOR

Therefore if I have seen something it is quite possible that there are many people who have not seen the same thing; and if it has interested me it is quite likely that others will be curious to see it also ?

PLAYGOER

It generally is so with people.

STAGE-DIRECTOR

You, for instance ?

PLAYGOER

Yes.

STAGE-DIRECTOR

Do you think I may be allowed to show it to you if I am able to do so ?

PLAYGOER

Certainly you may.

STAGE-DIRECTOR

If I do not show it to you you may never see it, so practically speaking, until I show you, it may be said to belong to me ?

PLAYGOER

We may admit so much.

STAGE-DIRECTOR

It belongs to me, then; and as it is not likely that I should desire to show you something which belongs to me in a damaged condition I must be very careful of the method I employ to transfer it from its situation to your presence. I must be practical ?

PLAYGOER

Yes, your method must be essentially practical if you wish to avoid all accidents.

STAGE-DIRECTOR

And by practical you mean—what ?

PLAYGOER

The meaning of the word practical is that which is possible of accomplishment.

STAGE-DIRECTOR

You are right. And is there but one way of accomplishing everything ?

PLAYGOER

No, there is generally more than one way. Why do you ask ?

STAGE-DIRECTOR

You must forgive me for the assumption, but my intention was to ascertain whether you confused the phrase the "practical way" with another phrase, the "usual way," or with a third, the "matter-of-fact way."

PLAYGOER

Most certainly not.

STAGE-DIRECTOR

Again forgive me; but to confuse the meaning of the word "practical" has become so usual lately, especially when speaking of the Theatre. Let us proceed: I was saying that if I had something which belonged to me and wanted to show it to you I must take great care, if I wished to bring it to you without in any way damaging it.

PLAYGOER

Yes.

STAGE-DIRECTOR

Of course we admit the supposition that I cannot take you to see it, and there are some things which are so situated. The North Pole, for instance; or an idea—and to all intents and purposes the North Pole is nothing more nor less than an idea. If I tell you, for instance, that I have seen the North Pole you are no more enlightened than if I told you I had seen Heaven.

PLAYGOER

True.

STAGE-DIRECTOR

Whereas if I tell you I have seen a church-steeple you have something familiar to go upon from which you can construct an actuality. The North Pole, or an idea, is something to which I cannot take you without *considerable exertion* on your part as well as my own; but I can convey an idea to you or a proof that the North Pole exists at a certain spot on the globe. But, as we agreed, it must be brought to you with great care. For instance, my proof of the existence of the North Pole must be made quite clear to you, and though this will give you no exertion whatever, it will give me exactly double as much as if you had gone with me to search for those proofs.

PLAYGOER

How is that ?

STAGE-DIRECTOR

You will remember that we agreed that the mere *telling* you I have seen the North Pole is not sufficient proof that I speak the truth, whereas the mere telling you that I have seen a church-steeple is enough.[1] Now, what would be enough to prove to you I had seen the North Pole ?

[1] To demand proof of all things great and small is always the sign of the little mind. But to demand proof of great things only and to accept the little is a sign of the smallest intellect. If demonstration is at all valuable it is entirely valuable. Is proof valueless? The question has never been answered.

PLAYGOER

You would have to prove before a group of experts and scientists by means of certain observations, etc.

STAGE-DIRECTOR

Would that prove the truth of my statement?

PLAYGOER

I suppose so; it is the test they go upon.

STAGE-DIRECTOR

And you, could I not prove it to you?

PLAYGOER

Well, no; you see I should not be able to understand you; my only chance of being in sympathy with your tale would be to trust in the experts before whom you had laid your proofs.

STAGE-DIRECTOR

But would my tale have any interest for you? could you have sympathy with what you could not understand?

PLAYGOER

Oh yes; yet it seems strange on thinking about it.

STAGE-DIRECTOR

Not so strange, and yet stranger than you suppose. The strangest part of it all is that man should be so lacking in natural instinct and moral courage. If we had preserved both, we would not ask for those *actual* proofs and we would believe and understand great truths the more easily. Anyhow, it is amusing as it is. Where we do not understand or believe, we become the children of those who can both believe and understand—that is as it should be, being as it is.

PLAYGOER

May I ask you——

STAGE-DIRECTOR

But come, let us get on. To believe in the idea which I bring you (this North Pole idea) you will rely upon the judgment of the wise men before whom I lay the proofs.

Those proofs are our little difficulty. In order to take observations and soundings, in order to bring back minerals, certain birds, plants, and such-like things which will prove my story I shall have to be very careful, very well equipped and well assisted. To travel into the unknown is to court disaster, and few set out without carefully organizing their equipment. Therefore ship, crew, instruments, all these things are selected only after the most cautious consideration. Neither too much nor too little of anything must be taken. On such a journey through an unknown land, and one in which so-called natural conditions so powerfully play the part of enemy, where Nature seems to defy one to pluck out the heart of her mystery, everything must be done to anticipate all emergencies.

Even when we have prepared everything with the greatest care accidents will still threaten the safety of our expedition.

We shall need enough of everything and not too much; therefore it is not a matter of money—although enough money is certainly necessary.

PLAYGOER

But what has this to do with the Theatre?

STAGE-DIRECTOR

Patience for a little and you will see.

We make these provisions after we have made our plan. That is the most difficult part of the work, for once made we must follow it to the end, while at the same time seizing the fresh opportunities as they present themselves.

Now that we are ready to start, consider for one instant what it is we are setting out to do. We are about to make a dangerous and very difficult expedition into the unknown to bring you back a few visible proofs of the known. We are not to bring back the idea itself, but only its fringe; for to return from the unknown with the idea itself would certainly make you think we were mad, whereas to bring back hints of the idea satisfies you as to our sanity.

PLAYGOER

What a strange paradox !

STAGE-DIRECTOR

Well, let us accept it; you want the pretty little fringe; you shall have it, although it is that fringe that costs so much to obtain which presents the whole difficulty. And now for the Theatre. But first a request.

PLAYGOER

What is it ?

STAGE-DIRECTOR

You asked me not to speak any more about temples or about the Art of the Theatre which I once told you was lost; which a beautiful poet well described to me as having " lain hid under the roots of the Pyramids for two thousand years, so solemn it is." Give me leave to speak again of this.

PLAYGOER

Will you speak to some practical purpose ?

STAGE-DIRECTOR

Only so.

PLAYGOER

You will not merely tell me what this art once meant to us, and what it should mean again, but you will show me a practical way of bringing it to us once more ?

STAGE-DIRECTOR

That is my intention.

PLAYGOER

You will not propose to destroy all the present theatres of the world in order to do this, for then I should not listen to you, for it would be no longer a practical proposition.

STAGE-DIRECTOR

No, I will not do so. How delighted I am to hear you express the wish that the present theatres shall in no way be injured! It shows me that your interest in them is reviving and that I have already nearly cured you. Remember, the Gaiety, 8 o'clock!

PLAYGOER

I have not forgotten. But now your practical plan?

STAGE-DIRECTOR

My proposal is to discover or rediscover the lost Art of the Theatre by a practical expedition, carried out swiftly and without unnecessary expense, into the realms where it lies hidden.

PLAYGOER

A good intention. And your method?

STAGE-DIRECTOR

The very simplest. It is based upon the methods

employed by Arctic explorers. The discovery of this art is the exact counterpart of the discovery of the North Pole.

Both are situated in the same position, in the unknown. We possess clues as to the whereabouts of both; both are shrouded in much mystery, both realms are themselves, by all reports, the very home of mystery and beauty.

In preparing for our first expedition (for we expect to make several) we shall follow the method employed by Nansen. First we shall take time—we shall take three or four years to make our preparations, and the scheme itself has already been in preparation for over six years.

So it was with Nansen's project.

Let me read you an extract from his *Farthest North*, which I have just been reading, relating to the plans and preparations for his expedition in 1893:

"If we turn our attention to the long list of former expeditions and to their equipments, it cannot but strike us that scarcely a single vessel has been built specially for the purpose—in fact, the majority of explorers have not even provided themselves with vessels which were originally intended for ice navigation.

"This is the more surprising when we remember the sums of money that have been lavished on the equipment of some of these expeditions. The fact is, they have generally been in such a hurry to set out that there has been no time to devote to a more careful equipment. In many cases, indeed, preparations were not begun until a few months before the expedition sailed. The present expedition, however, could not be equipped in so short a time, and if the voyage itself took three years the preparations took no less time, while the scheme was conceived thrice three years earlier.

"Plan after plan did Archer make of the projected ship; one model after another was prepared and abandoned.

"Fresh improvements were constantly being suggested. The form we finally adhered to may seem to many people by no means beautiful, but that it is well adapted to the ends in view I think our expedition has fully proved."

Here you see what long and careful preparation was made before the setting out of the expedition.

PLAYGOER

Yes, and also much money was needed, as I suppose it will be for your scheme?

STAGE-DIRECTOR

Certainly we shall need support, financial as well as moral, and we shall get it.

PLAYGOER

How do you know this?

STAGE-DIRECTOR

Patience a little; I shall come to the matter of expense in due time. When we have our scheme well supported—and £5000 a year guaranteed for five years will be all we shall require—we shall put the following plan into action.

We shall build and equip a college, furnishing it with what is necessary.

It will have to contain two theatres, one open-air and one roofed-in. These two stages, closed and open, are necessary for our experiments, and on one or on the other, sometimes on both, every theory shall be tested and records made of the results.

These records will be written, drawn, photographed or registered on the cinematograph or gramophone for future reference, but they will not be made public and will be only for the use of members of the college.

Other instruments for the study of natural sound and light will be purchased, together with the instruments for producing these artificially, and will lead us to the better knowledge of both sound and light, and also to the invention of yet better instruments through which the purer beauty of both sound and light may be passed.

In addition, instruments will be purchased for the study of motion, and some will be especially invented for this purpose.

To this equipment we shall add a printing-press,

all kinds of carpenters' tools, a well-stocked library, and all things pertaining to modern theatres. With these materials and instruments we shall pursue the study of the Stage as it is to-day with the intention of finding out those weaknesses which have brought it to its present unfortunate condition. We shall, in short, experiment upon the body of the modern theatre in our roofed-in theatre (for you will remember we have two), exactly in the same way as surgeons and their pupils experiment upon the bodies of dead men and animals.

In selecting its method of administration the college will follow the ancient precedent of Nature. It will consist of a head, a body and its members, the leader being selected by election. Those who are to compose the executive body are less difficult to decide on, as their task is undoubtedly less difficult.

In all there will not be more than thirty men in the college. There will be no women.

So now, are you clear as to these two points? First, that we shall have a college of experiment in which to study the three natural sources of art—Sound, Light and Motion—or, as I have spoken of them elsewhere, *voice*, *scene* and *action*.

Secondly, that we shall number in all thirty working-men, who shall singly and together pursue the study of the three subjects named and the other experiments to test the principles of the modern theatre. Is that clear to you?

PLAYGOER

It is. But how does your actual work resemble that of an Arctic explorer ?

STAGE-DIRECTOR

In this way. We shall have to select a centre from which search-parties shall be sent in different directions, our object being to explore within reason any part of the theatrical world which is unknown to us. We shall at the same time go over much old ground in the belief that it has never been thoroughly examined. No great hopes are entertained of finding there anything of great value, but an examination is necessary. As soon as possible we shall push forward in the direction of the unknown. Just as search-parties are sent in a certain direction with instructions to sound and make observations and then to return to the point selected as a base, so will our investigators push forward their studies into certain regions from which, when they have fully explored them and collected sufficient evidence, they will return to the point where they had separated from us to make known the result of their observations.

If this work proceed as rapidly as we hope, we shall advance to a new position at which to establish our base within the first year. On the other hand, it may prove to be more difficult, in which case we shall have to stay where we are.

Above all I wish to emphasize this point: that no change of base shall ever be made until every one is fully assured of the practicality of the next position.

You will understand that our reason for pushing forward our base is to facilitate communication in the event of our search-parties pushing far into the unknown. By this method, and with sufficient supplies, we can make attempt on attempt, to compass our end. It is the only method which suggests itself to me, and I cannot think of a more practical one, for you must remember that acting on such a plan guarantees continual success of one kind or another. Call to mind how many important observations and records were made, not only by those who went farthest north, but by those who searched even in those latitudes into which many men had travelled before.

At the end of a year our books will hold the records of things hitherto undiscovered, dates and results of experiments of incalculable value—not only to us in our future efforts, but to those who shall resume the search when we may be obliged to abandon it.

PLAYGOER

Then you think it likely your efforts will not meet with all the success you could desire?

STAGE-DIRECTOR

On the contrary—I think we can be sure of exceptional success; as to any *final* success, it is a rare thing to achieve, for finality is something which probably does not exist. Now tell me, does my plan and its method of execution appeal to you?

PLAYGOER

Let me try to say what I think. The plan is an ideal one, and, as your quest is ideal, is in harmony with that for which you search. But will you find support? Will you, to begin with, find the support of the leaders of the Theatrical Profession?

STAGE-DIRECTOR

Whom do you mean?

PLAYGOER

Well, to be outspoken, Sir Herbert Tree, Sir Charles Wyndham, Arthur Bourchier, Weedon Grossmith, Cyril Maude——

STAGE-DIRECTOR

The actor-managers, you mean?

PLAYGOER

Yes, but I had not finished my list of names, which includes not only all those connected with the arts in England and even some of those connected with the State, but also certain names of artists abroad. For instance, will the Theatre in Europe support you—the French theatre, either the Comédie Française or one of the smaller representative theatres such as those directed by Bernhardt or Antoine? Will the German theatre give you any support? The State theatres, or Reinhardt, for instance, or the Munchen Art Theatre? Holland—what can Holland do? and Sweden, Russia or Italy? The Constan Art Theatre about which you have told me, or Eleonora Duse, about whose ideals I have heard so much? And then the Americans? You see, I want to know on whom you rely for support, for that is the first requisite to make your scheme practical.

STAGE-DIRECTOR

You have put me an easy question to answer. You have mentioned some of the best-known names in the theatrical world. If the proposed college is opposed to all their interests they will not support it. But consider whether this is the case. For instance, amongst those you have named are possibly a few men of decidedly ideal tendencies. The directors of the Constan Art Theatre are undoubtedly such men. I think we have their support. Madame Duse? I think she would never refuse hers. Then there is Reinhardt of Berlin. Such a scheme is one which is certainly not opposed to his interests. And that Sir Herbert Beerbohm-

Tree's name will be found in such company is far more likely than that he should join issue with those weary gentlemen whose love of adventure has left them. Madame Bernhardt and Antoine are more than likely to applaud our proposals and to guarantee them as practical if they read and understand them.

PLAYGOER

And will these do no more than give you their *moral* support ?

STAGE-DIRECTOR

Why, what else can they give ? They are hard workers in a very different profession, and already their reputation for generosity has been too often imposed upon. If they will give us their hands and bid us God-speed it is all we should ever dream of asking for.

PLAYGOER

Well, but your capital—where is that coming from ? A bundle of God-speeds are pretty, but no practical use can be made of them.

STAGE-DIRECTOR

You may be right, though everything is not valued by making a practical use of it. We shall expect to receive practical support from the State.

PLAYGOER

Your confidence inspires me to believe you are right. But there are two things which you will have to prove to the State before it will accord you its support.

STAGE-DIRECTOR

What are they ?

PLAYGOER

First, you will have to show clearly that the State would benefit; secondly, that the advantage would exceed the cost.

STAGE-DIRECTOR

Very well, then, let us first consider how the State would benefit.

The Theatre affects the people in two different ways. It either instructs or it amuses. There are many ways to instruct and to amuse. Now, which would you say was the more instructive, something heard or something seen ?

PLAYGOER

I would say the latter.

STAGE-DIRECTOR

And which would you say was easier of comprehension, the beautiful or the ugly, the noble or the mean ?

PLAYGOER

If we seek for instruction it is easier to comprehend the beautiful and the noble, for it is that which we are searching for; if we seek for amusement the ignoble and ugly is possibly more immediate in its effect.

STAGE-DIRECTOR

And is the beautiful and the noble more amusing ?

PLAYGOER

I think it is not.

STAGE-DIRECTOR

And yet what is that which, when you see and hear it, causes you to feel smilingly from top to toe ?

PLAYGOER

The beautiful—truth—oh, something which it is quite beyond us to explain.

STAGE-DIRECTOR

I think so too. Yet is there not something of amusement in it? for we smile; and a smile is the whisper of laughter.

PLAYGOER

You are right.

STAGE-DIRECTOR

Perhaps we may call it the very best part of amusement ?

PLAYGOER

We may for the sake of argument.

STAGE-DIRECTOR

And this is connected, as we have seen, with the beautiful and the noble; therefore the very best part of amusement is akin to the best part of instruction.

PLAYGOER

It seems so.

STAGE-DIRECTOR

Now, we have said that the Theatre *either* instructs or amuses. Yet we see that sometimes it acts in both ways; in short, it both instructs *and* amuses when it is noblest and most beautiful.

PLAYGOER

True.

STAGE-DIRECTOR

Would you say that this feeling, which for want of the right word I have called "smiling from top to toe," is a good or a bad feeling?

PLAYGOER

I should say it was the very best feeling.

STAGE-DIRECTOR

In fact, if you saw hundreds of faces in a gathering of people wreathed in smiles, you would say that they felt happier than if you saw those faces strained and weary-looking?

PLAYGOER

Why, certainly I should.

STAGE-DIRECTOR

And tell me, if you were a king, would you rather see happy faces such as I have described or gloomy ones ?

PLAYGOER

Happy ones, of course.

STAGE-DIRECTOR

Another question : Would you prefer to see them smiling or thoughtful ?

PLAYGOER

Smiling or thoughtful ? The thoughtful face is not necessarily the gloomy face,—and yet I would prefer that they smiled.

STAGE-DIRECTOR

Why would you prefer it ?

PLAYGOER

Because then I too should feel like smiling.

STAGE-DIRECTOR

A good answer. Now you told me just now that something *seen* instructs us more than something *heard*. May I take it that you mean that what we see is more swiftly and more easily comprehended ?

PLAYGOER

Yes, that is what I mean.

STAGE-DIRECTOR

Let us take an example. We see a finely bred horse let loose in a field. He gambols, arches his neck, looks around splendidly with his eye. If we had never seen a horse before, no description would convey the right impression to us so swiftly as does this *seeing* him.

PLAYGOER

Yes, that is very true.

STAGE-DIRECTOR

And would a verbal description of the horse delivered at the same time as it became visible to us assist us to understand better what we see?

PLAYGOER

No, I think it might confuse us, for we should be so much occupied in gazing at the creature.

STAGE-DIRECTOR

Then you would not be prepared to *hear* anything about it in addition to seeing it?

PLAYGOER

No, it would rather irritate than assist.

STAGE-DIRECTOR

And yet they say that instruction is obtained

through the sense of hearing as well as through that of sight.

PLAYGOER

Yes, but the two impressions are likely to confound each other if they come to us simultaneously.

STAGE-DIRECTOR

Well, then, let us put it differently. Suppose the horse in his gambols before us should give expression to his joy and pride by neighing—what then ?

PLAYGOER

Ah, that's true ! That would assist us to comprehend; our senses would be delighted.

STAGE-DIRECTOR

The neigh of a horse, then, is more illuminating than a learned discourse ? Would you smile on hearing it ?

PLAYGOER

Yes, it is very likely.

STAGE-DIRECTOR

You would say then that you had been *perfectly* instructed, for you had seen something noble and you had heard some playful expression proceeding from that which seemed so noble, and you would smile through your understanding. You would not become thoughtful, would you ?

PLAYGOER

No, no; I should be enchanted.

STAGE-DIRECTOR

You would; and that is precisely the state of mind you achieve in a theatre such as I mentioned, where instruction and amusement spring from the contemplation by eye and ear of the beautiful. You would be *enchanted.* A poorer state of mind would be the result should instruction without amusement be offered you; you would be merely instructed. And a much poorer state of mind would result if you received amusement without instruction.

You will bear in mind that I have all along spoken of true amusement in a high sense and true instruction in the same sense; that is to say, I have spoken of them as two things which it is possible and desirable to connect, and therefore have indicated that they are very much alike and indeed hardly divisible.

PLAYGOER

Yet they are separated, for the music-hall echoes with shrieks and howls of the loudest laughter, and the faces of the audience at the Lyceum are very much drawn during the performance of *King Lear* or *Hamlet.*

STAGE-DIRECTOR

Yes, that is precisely what I am wanting to talk

about. The division is much too great, especially in England, for in a music hall in Germany we hear far fewer bursts of rough laughter, and the faces at the tragedies are less strained and more thoughtful. A perfect theatre would neither tighten nor loosen the muscles of the face, and would neither contract the cells of the brain nor the heart-strings. All would be set at ease; and to produce this state of mental and physical ease in the people is the duty of the Theatre and its Art.

PLAYGOER

But a perfect theatre is impossible.

STAGE-DIRECTOR

What do I hear? What is it you say? I think we are in England—no? I think you are an Englishman—am I right? and I think you will withdraw that last remark of yours at once.

PLAYGOER

You look so like that horse you were describing that I do so to avoid your heels!

STAGE-DIRECTOR

Bravo! And now that it is agreed that it is possible to create a perfect theatre here in England let us see how we may do so. You say we must prove that the State will be benefited before we can hope for its support. Well, it is the most perfect theatre in the world that we shall offer to the State, and is not that a benefit? This theatre will be created after some years of toil [1] by following the method of search which I have sketched out for you.

PLAYGOER

But you have not shown me that the cost of this "expedition" will be less than the advantage to the State, which will only be benefited if the gain exceeds the expense.

STAGE-DIRECTOR

I will do so in as few words as possible; though, in a short conversation, I cannot bring all the proof to bear upon this and other points that I could do if the matter should be taken up for more serious inquiry by a committee appointed for the purpose.

The expenses of our first five years would be, as I said before, £25,000. Now, £25,000 possibly seems to you a great deal of money. Let us see, however, what it really represents.

It represents F. Nansen's expenses for his Polar Expedition, 1893–96.

It represents the cost of one picture in the National Gallery.

It represents the cost of about three to five

[1] The Constan Art Theatre, the most perfectly organized and conducted theatre in Europe, has taken ten years to achieve its present perfection, and only in the tenth year did it commence to return a dividend.

productions at His Majesty's Theatre or Drury Lane.

It represents about the cost of a single Pageant in England, 1908.

It represents one quarter of Sarah Bernhardt's profits for her tour in France, 1880–81.

It represents the average takings of a hundred London theatres for one night.

It represents about a third of the sum paid for a single "Triumph" in 1634.[1]

It represents less than half the sum spent on enlarging and improving the Lyceum Theatre in 1881.

It represents a fifth of the profits of one single Irving tour in America.[2]

Now tell me, do you think £25,000 a large sum to pay for the expenses of so important a work covering five years?

PLAYGOER

I do not think so now after what you have told me.

STAGE-DIRECTOR

Now consider, also, how much the *public* has to pay for the many theatrical experiments made every year. You may say that nearly every production in London and the provinces is to-day an

[1] "The Triumph of Peace." See SYMONDS: *Shakespeare's Predecessors*, p. 27.

[2] BRERETON: *Life of Irving*, p. 312.

experiment—an honest if incomplete and methodless experiment—towards bettering the craft of stage work. The public is led to believe that these experiments are finished works of art, whereas they are not works of art at all, but just honestly intended, though shockingly perpetrated, *blunders*.

Now would it not be cheaper for the public if some one—the State, a millionaire, or even the public itself—should pay such a small sum as I have indicated, £25,000, to cover the expenses of five years' serious and practical experiment by picked men, rather than to continue for ever to part yearly with the sum of £2,500,000 (two millions and a half sterling), as it is doing to-day, for experiments made in a hurry and without method ?

PLAYGOER

Does the public part with so great a sum yearly ?

STAGE-DIRECTOR

Let us see if I am correct. Let us say that there are one hundred theatres in England.[1] Let us say each of the hundred takes £250 a night from the public,[2] and let us say they take this for one hundred nights as representing a year.[3]

We place the whole calculation as low as possible, and it still reaches a colossal total of *two millions and a half sterling, taken from the public in the*

[1] There are more than six times that number.
[2] The Lyceum in 1881 could hold £328 in one evening.
[3] Theatres remain open for over two hundred nights in a year.

course of one year for rubbish. Have I answered your second question, then?

PLAYGOER

Hardly. I asked you if the advantage to be derived by the State would exceed the cost. You have only shown me that the cost is exceedingly low in comparison with other State and private expenditures, but you have yet to show me that the State will reap its £25,000 worth of advantages.

STAGE-DIRECTOR

Let us look into that at once. The State will receive from the college at the end of five years the results of their labours. These will include: (1) A practical demonstration of the best method to be employed for building and directing a national theatre as an ideal theatre, and in a manner hitherto deemed impossible. (2) The improvement by simplification of many of the mechanical appliances of the modern stage. (3) The training of stage-managers and of the staff employed to shift the scenery. (4) The training of actors to speak and to move—the chief difficulties of the average actor. (5) The training of a group of original scene-painters, a group of perfectly drilled men to execute any given order regarding the lights on the Stage, for at present, as any visit to a special light rehearsal will show, the lighting staff in a theatre is always at sea.

There are three main reasons for this; the first is that a stage-director does not know what he wants, does not know the names or uses of the machines employed or of their parts or what these machines are capable of, and is utterly ignorant of how to obtain a result. He leaves it all to accident and chance "effect." The second reason is that the majority of men who work the machines at evening performances are employed on different work by day, and have received but the barest training as to their duties. The third reason is that the machines are designed without knowledge of the use to which they should serve. Still, it must be admitted that the electricians have many unnecessary difficulties to contend with, which would be removed if the whole craft of the modern stage were to be studied afresh with a view to readjusting its component parts. There is only one man to whom we look for this—the stage-manager; but his opportunities of study are few, for his time is occupied in having to attend to and straighten out awkward situations, created too often by the director of the theatre and by the actors, actresses and supers. If he attempts to improve things every one loses their heads. When the stage-manager can have time to train, and can afterwards be given authority and opportunity to train his staff, theatres will take a small step in the right direction. A college is the only place where such training can be received and given.

In short, what we should tender to the State in return for its support, would be the nucleus of an Ideal Theatre on a practical basis, with a college for the subsequent training of the staff from stage-manager to electricians, raising all to an ideal standard which should not be lowered under any excuse whatever.

You see then that the college, with its eyes fixed on the future and its ideal firmly established, would keep its hands and fingers busy with the present. The search for the lost Art of the Theatre must be made only after passing through the regions in which the modern theatre is situated. In passing we shall re-establish its order; do you understand ?

PLAYGOER

I think you have made it clear. And now, one more question. Are you to act as the head of this college ?

STAGE-DIRECTOR

No. The head, or leader, as I tell you, will be elected by the members.

PLAYGOER

And will you not enter for election ? What will the college be without you ?

STAGE-DIRECTOR

Everything. With me, nothing.

PLAYGOER

What do you mean? Will you desert the very scheme you have created?

STAGE-DIRECTOR

No; I shall never be absent from the college, but I shall not act as either head, body or member.

PLAYGOER

What will you do, then?

STAGE-DIRECTOR

I shall give it its existence, and shall then ask to be permitted free entrance to the college, so as to study there whenever I wish to. And my reasons for desiring this are many. To explain them to you fully would take many years. But you may take it that they are not lazy reasons. I should feel honoured to be a member of such a college.

PLAYGOER

But you will give it more than this—you will yourself make experiments and lend your gifts to the work?

STAGE-DIRECTOR

My gifts are few and cannot be lent. I would willingly make experiments if asked to do so, but I believe I can be of more use to this college at a little distance than connected with it.

PLAYGOER

And this is how you would propose to discover this lost art, which you, probably, more than any one else, know most about?

STAGE-DIRECTOR

I know very little about it, but possibly I know where it is situated better than the others. I can point to the right direction, and for this reason I believe I am not altogether valueless to the efforts of the college. In their search, their experiments, I shall be ever with them, but I shall not lead them, nor must I be expected to follow them. Whenever called upon I shall be at their service, but not for any fixed occupation.

PLAYGOER

Well, you somewhat take my breath away. You prove to me that you know as much or more than the rest of the world about this Third Art, as you have called it, and you talk about it to me for hours; you give up everything in your life for it and you propose to plan out the college up to a certain point—and then you hand over your college, idea, plan, to some one else. Have you no fear that the whole thing will become much changed when it leaves your hands?

STAGE-DIRECTOR

It will certainly change—its existence depends upon this fact; but I have no fear because of that.

PLAYGOER

But have you no personal desires in relation to this college? Will you not be a little pained to see it moving in a wrong direction?

STAGE-DIRECTOR

It will not do so. The magnet of the ideal is fixed; attraction has already commenced; it is in resisting this that we shall make our discoveries. There will be men with us who will from time to time become depressed and tired, and then mistakes are likely to occur—and with the mistakes discoveries. But the mistakes will never be wilfully made from some selfish motive, and can but be the result of too great a strain. But these resistances, as I said, will only lead us towards our ideal.

PLAYGOER

But the modern theatre which you profess to despise resists the attraction of the ideal.

STAGE-DIRECTOR

Ah! that is quite different. They resist through fear; we shall resist through courage. We shall hear the call and feel the pull, and we shall go straight onwards, but with slow deliberation, making discoveries all along the way. We shall finally discover what we look for and what attracts us, and then——

"HUNGER." A Drama

The Prologue.

I once wrote, or rather constructed, a Drama called "Hunger," making for it many designs. I hope to complete this Drama when I have my school and workmen to help me. For to finish a thing for the stage in the study is a mistake I ought not to be guilty of.

And then I hope to give performances of it before a small and select audience.

Not that I believe the theatre is for the "few"— but there are some plays and some shows which are not for "the many." Nothing would make me alter or destroy this Drama—but nothing would persuade me that it would be right to show it to a large and mixed audience.

For it is wrong for the poor and hungry to be shown *a vision of themselves and their misery—but it is not entirely wrong to show it to a few people who might, if they once* saw, *do something to make Hunger less general.*

No amount of preaching in a theatre is of any more use to humanity than preaching in the streets. For words never explain. But to see *a thing, and how sad some things are and how terrible other things are, is quite a different matter. Argument is silenced. In my Drama the Hunger of the Poor and the Hunger of the Rich were placed side by side. And the king or man of God stood apart—and no one could tell us what he felt—As it always was and always will be.*

"HUNGER." A Drama

The Prologue.

I once wrote, or rather constructed, a Drama called "Hunger," *making for it many designs. I hope to complete this Drama when I have my school and workmen to help me. For to finish a thing for the stage in the study is a mistake I ought not to be guilty of.*

And then I hope to give performances of it before a small and select audience.

Not that I believe the theatre is for the "few"—but there are some plays and some shows which are not for "the many." Nothing would make me alter or destroy this Drama—but nothing would persuade me that it would be right to show it to a large and mixed audience.

For it is wrong for the poor and hungry to be shown a vision of themselves and their misery—but it is not entirely wrong to show it to a few people who might, if they once saw, do something to make Hunger less general.

No amount of preaching in a theatre is of any more use to humanity than preaching in the streets. For words never explain. But to see a thing, and how sad some things are and how terrible other things are, is quite a different matter. Argument is silenced. In my Drama the Hunger of the Poor and the Hunger of the Rich were placed side by side. And the king or man of God stood apart—and no one could tell us what he felt—As it always was and always will be.

[*Face page 262.*

PLAYGOER

What then ?

STAGE-DIRECTOR

A question. And for my part I am thoroughly convinced that there will never be an end to our journey. Attraction shall never cease for us; that will never change, we shall ever be invited, beckoned, impelled to move forward.

1910.

ON THE GHOSTS IN THE TRAGEDIES OF SHAKESPEARE

A VERY curious indication as to the way in which the producer should treat the Shakespearean tragedies on the stage lies in the appearance in those tragedies of the ghosts or spirits.

The fact of their presence precludes a realistic treatment of the tragedies in which they appear. Shakespeare has made them the centre of his vast dreams, and the central point of a dream, as of a circular geometrical figure, controls and conditions every hair's breadth of the circumference.

These spirits set the key to which, as in music, every note of the composition must be harmonized; they are integral, not extraneous parts of the drama; they are the visualized symbols of the supernatural world which enfolds the natural, exerting in the action something of that influence which in "the science of sound" is exerted by those "partial tones, which are unheard, but which blend with the tones which are heard and make all the difference between the poorest instrument and the supreme note of a violin"; for, as with these, "so in the science of life, in the crowded street or market place or theatre, or wherever life is, there are partial tones, there are unseen presences. Side by side with the human crowd is a crowd of unseen forms.

Principalities and Powers and Possibilities. . . . These are unseen but not unfelt. They enter into the houses of the human beings that are seen, and for their coming some of them are swept and garnished, and they abide there, and the last state of these human beings is radiant with a divine light and resonant with an added love; or, on the contrary, it may be that, haunted by spirits more wicked than themselves, the last state of such beings is worse than before: subject to a violence and tyranny abhorrent even to themselves; impalpable and inevitable as it would seem, even to the confines of despair."

It is by the necromancy of these "partial tones," by the introduction of influences felt even when unseen, at times impalpable as the "shadow of a shadow," yet realized even then as dominant forces, sometimes malefic, sometimes beneficent, that Shakespeare achieves results which surpass those of his contemporaries even when, like Middleton in his *Witch*, they treat of similar themes.

For when Shakespeare wrote, "enter the ghost of Banquo," he did not have in his mind merely a player clothed in a piece of gauze. Nor had he done so, had he been preoccupied with gauze and limelight, would he ever have created the Ghost in *Hamlet*; for that ghost of Hamlet's father, who moves aside the veils at the beginning of the great

[1] Shorthouse.

play, is not a joke; he is not a theatrical gentleman in armour, is not a farce of a figure. He is a momentary visualization of the unseen forces which dominate the action and is a clear command from Shakespeare that the men of the theatre shall rouse their imagination and let their reasonable logic slumber.

For the appearances of all these spirits in the plays are not the inventions of a pantomime manager; they are the loftiest achievements of a lofty poet, and carry to us the clearest statements we can ever receive as to Shakespeare's thoughts about the stage.

"The suggestive shall predominate, for all pictures on the stage pretending to illusionize reality must necessarily fail in their effect or cause a disillusionment. Shakespeare's dramas are poetic creations and must be presented and treated as such;"[1] advice which should be especially borne in mind by all who set themselves to interpret those of the plays in which the supernatural element is introduced.

Thus if a man of the theatre shall produce *Macbeth*, *Hamlet*, *Richard the Third*, *Julius Cæsar*, *Antony and Cleopatra*, *The Tempest*, or *A Midsummer Night's Dream* as they should be produced, he must first of all woo the spirits in those plays; for unless he understand them with his whole being he shall but produce a thing of rags and tatters.

[1] Hevesi.

The moment, however, that he is at one with these spirits, the moment he has seen their proportion and moved to their rhythm, in that moment is he a master of the art of producing a play by Shakespeare. But this the stage-manager never seems to realize, for did he do so he would adopt a very different method for the interpretation of those scenes in which the ghosts appear.

For what is it makes the ghosts of Shakespeare, which are so significant and impressive when we read the plays, appear so weak and unconvincing on the stage? It is because in the latter case the tap is turned on suddenly, the right atmosphere has not been prepared.

Enter a ghost—sudden panic of all the actors, of all the limelights, of all the music and of the entire audience. Exit the ghost—intense relief of the whole theatre. In fact, with the exit of the ghost on the stage the audience may be said to feel that something best not spoken about has been passed over. And so the mighty question, which is at the roots of the whole world, of life and death, that fine theme ever productive of so much beauty and from which Shakespeare weaves his veils, is slurred over, avoided as with an apologetic cough.

We are children in such matters. We think a bogie will do. We giggle when we are asked to present the idea of something spiritual, for we know nothing of spirits, disbelieving in them. We giggle like children and wrap ourselves in a table-cloth and say "Wow, wow, wow." Yet consider such plays as *Hamlet, Macbeth, Richard the Third.* What is it gives them their supreme mystery and terror, which raises them above mere tragedies of ambition, murder, madness and defeat? Is it not just that supernatural element which dominates the action from first to last; that blending of the material and the mystical; that sense of waiting figures intangible as death, of mysterious featureless faces of which, sideways, we seem to catch a glimpse, although, on turning fully round, we find nothing there? In *Macbeth* the air is thick with mystery, the whole action ruled by an invisible power; and it is just those words which are never heard, just those figures which seldom shape themselves more definitely than a cloud's shadow, that give the play its mysterious beauty, its splendour, its depth and immensity, and in which lies its primary tragic element.

Let the stage-manager concentrate his attention and that of his audience on the seen things which are temporal, and such a play is robbed of half its majesty and all its significance. But let him introduce, without travesty, the supernatural element; raise the action from the merely material to the psychological, and render audible to the ears of the soul if not of the body "the solemn uninterrupted whisperings of man and his destiny," point out "the uncertain dolorous footsteps of the being, as he approaches, or wanders from, his truth, his beauty or his God," and show how, underlying *King Lear, Macbeth* and *Hamlet,* is "the murmur of eternity on the horizon,"[1] and he will be fulfilling the poet's intention instead of turning his majestic spirits into sepulchral-voiced gentlemen with whitened faces and robes of gauze.

Consider, for instance, more in detail, the play of *Macbeth,* in which "the overwhelming pressure of preternatural agency urges on the tide of human passion with redoubled force."[2] The whole success of its representation depends upon the power of the stage-manager to suggest this preternatural agency and on the capacity of the actor to submit to the tide of the play, to that mysterious mesmerism which masters Macbeth and his "troop of friends."

I seem to see him in the first four acts of the play as a man who is hypnotized, seldom moving, but, when he does so, moving as a sleep-walker. Later on in the play the places are changed, and Lady Macbeth's sleep-walking is like the grim, ironical echo of Macbeth's whole life, a sharp, shrill echo quickly growing fainter, fainter, and gone.

In the last act Macbeth awakes. It almost seems to be a new rôle. Instead of a sleep-walker dragging his feet heavily he becomes an ordinary man startled from a dream to find the dream true. He is not the man some actors show him to be, the trapped, cowardly villain; nor yet is he to my mind the

[1] Maeterlinck. [2] Hazlitt.

bold, courageous villain as other actors play him. He is as a doomed man who has been suddenly awakened on the morning of his execution, and, in the sharpness and abruptness of that awakening, understands nothing but the facts before him, and even of these understands the external meaning only. He sees the army in front of him; he will fight, and he prepares to do so, puzzling all the time about the meaning of his dream. Occasionally he relapses into his state of somnambulism. While his wife lived he was not conscious of his state, he acted the part of her medium perfectly, and she in her turn acted as medium to the spirits whose duty it ever is to test the strength of men by playing with their force upon the weakness of women.

Nietzsche, writing of Macbeth, sees only the mad ambition of the man, this human passion of ambition; and he tells us that this sight, instead of irresistibly detracting from the evil ambition in us, rather augments it. Perhaps this is so; but it seems to me that behind all this there is much more than evil ambition and the idea of the hero and the villain.

Behind it all I seem to perceive the unseen forces already spoken of; those spirits that Shakespeare was always so fond of hinting stood behind all things of this earth, moved them, and moved them apparently to these great deeds for good or evil.

In *Macbeth* they are called by the old grand-

MACBETH

A WITCH.—ACT. IV. SCENE I.

2nd Witch. *Fillet of a fenny snake;*
In the cauldron boil and bake;
Eye of newt, and toe of frog,
Wool of bat, and tongue of dog,
Adder's fork, and blind-worm's sting
Lizard's leg, and howlet's wing,
For a charm of powerful trouble,
Like a hell-broth boil and bubble.

All. *Double, double, toil and trouble;*
Fire, burn; and, cauldron, bubble.

[*Face page* 270

mother's title of the Three Witches, that elastic name which the public in the theatre may either laugh at or be serious about as it wishes.

Now when I speak of this hypnotic influence of these spirits as though I were mentioning something quite new, I am speaking entirely in relation to the interpretation of Shakespeare on the stage and not merely as his student. I know that the students have written about these spirits, comparing them to certain figures in the Greek tragedy and writing of them far more profoundly than I can do. But their writings are for those who read Shakespeare, or who see him acted, not for those who take part in the presentation of his plays. Whether the plays were ever intended to be acted or no, whether or not they gain by being acted, does not concern me here. But if I were asked to present this play of *Macbeth* upon the stage, I should need to bring to it an understanding different entirely from that which the student brings when he has only himself to consider as he sits reading it in private. You may feel the presence of these witches as you read the play, but which of you has ever felt their presence when you saw the play acted? And therein lies the failure of the producer and the actor.

In *Macbeth* it is, to my mind, during the hypnotic moments that we should feel the overpowering force of these unseen agencies; and how to make this felt, how to make it clear and yet not actual, is the problem of the stage-manager. To me it seems that the play has never yet been properly performed because we have never yet felt these spirits working through the woman at the man, and to achieve this would be one of the most difficult tasks which could be set the stage-manager, though not because of the difficulty of purchasing gauze which should be sufficiently transparent, not because of the difficulty of finding machinery capable of raising the ghosts, or any other such reason. The chief difficulty lies with the two performers of the rôles of Lady Macbeth and Macbeth, for if it is admitted that this spiritual element which Shakespeare called the Witches and Ghosts is in any way connected with the pain of these two beings, Macbeth and his Lady, then these two characters must show this to the audience.

But, while it rests with the actors of these two parts, it also rests with the actors of the witches, and above all with the stage-manager, to bring these spirits and their mediums into effective harmony.

On the stage the spirits are never seen during the scenes of Lady Macbeth, neither are we conscious of their influence; yet as we read the play we are not only conscious of the influence of these "sightless substances"; we are somehow conscious of their presence. We feel it as the presence of the French Abbé was felt in Shorthouse's romance of *The Countess Eve*.

Are there not moments in the play when one of these three spirits seems to have clapped its skinny hand upon Lady Macbeth's mouth and answered in her stead ? And who was it, if not one of them, who drew her by the wrist as she passed into the room of the old king with the two daggers in her hand ? Who was it pushed her by the elbow as she smeared the faces of the grooms ? Again, what is this dagger that Macbeth sees in the air ? by what thread of hair does it hang ? who dangles it ? and whose is the voice heard as he returns from the chamber of the murdered king ?

> *Macb.* I've done the deed. Didst thou not hear a noise?
> *Lady M.* I heard the owl scream and the crickets cry.
> Did not you speak?
> *Macb.* When?
> *Lady M.* Now.
> *Macb.* As I descended?

Who is this that was heard to speak as he descended ?

And who are these mysterious three who dancc gaily without making any sound around this miserable pair as they talk together in the dark after the dark deed ? We know quite well as we read; we forget altogether when we see the play presented upon the stage. There we see only the weak man being egged on by the ambitious woman who is assuming the manners of what is called the "Tragedy Queen"; and in other scenes we see the same man, having found that the same ambitious lady does not assist him, calling upon some bogies and having an interview with them in a cavern.

What we *should* see is a man in that hypnotic state which can be both terrible and beautiful to witness. We should realize that this hypnotism is transmitted to him through the medium of his wife, and we should recognize the witches as spirits, more terrible because more beautiful than we can conceive except by making them terrible. We should see them, not as Hazlitt imagined them, as "hags of mischief, obscene panderers to iniquity, malicious from their impotence of enjoyment, enamoured of destruction, because they are themselves unreal, abortive, half-existences, who become sublime from their exemption from all human sympathies and contempt for all human affairs," but rather picture them to ourselves as we picture the militant Christ scourging the money-lenders, the fools who denied Him. Here we have the idea of the supreme God, the supreme Love, and it is that which has to be brought into *Macbeth* on the stage. We see in this instance the God of Force as exemplified in these witches, placing these two pieces of mortality upon the anvil and crushing them because they were not hard enough to resist; consuming them because they could not stand the fire: offering the woman a crown for her husband, flattering her beyond measure, whispering to her of her superior force, of her superior intellect; whispering to him of his bravery.

See how persuasively the spirits can work upon the man or the woman when separated and alone! listen to the flow of their language; they are drunk with the force of these spirits though unaware of their presence

But note the moment when these two come together. In each other's faces they see, as it were, something so strange that they seem to be surprised by a reminiscence. "Where have I seen that before or felt that which I now see?" Each becomes furtive, alert, fearful, on the defensive, and so there is no outpouring of speech here, but their meeting is like the cautious approach of two animals.

What is it they see?—the spirit which clings round the feet or hangs upon the neck, or, as in the old Durer picture, is whispering in the ear? Yet why, one wonders, should these spirits appear so horrible when a moment ago we were speaking of them as beings so divine as to resemble the militant Christ? and the answer seems obvious. Is it not possible that the spirit may take as many forms as the body, as many forms as thought? These spirits are the many souls of nature, inexorable to the weak, yet obedient to those who obey.

But now let us come to the appearance of Banquo at the feast.

The whole play leads up to, and down from, this point. It is here that are pronounced the most terrible words heard during the play, here that is offered the most amazing impression for the eye. And in order to reach this moment decently, intelligently, that is to say, artistically, the figures must not walk about on the ground for the first two acts and suddenly appear on stilts in the third act or line, for then a great truth will appear as a great lie, Banquo's ghost as nothing.

We must open this play high up in an atmosphere loftier than that in which we generally grope, and which is a matter-of-fact, put-on-your-boots atmosphere; for this is a matter of fancy, a matter of that strangely despised thing, the imagination; that which we call the spiritual.

We should be conscious of the desire of the spirit to see the woman utterly annihilated herself rather than submit to the influence which this spirit brings upon the flesh as a test. We should see the horror of the spirit on perceiving the triumph of this influence.

Instead, we see of all this nothing on the stage. We do not know why the witches are worrying these two people; we feel that it is rather unpleasant. But that is not the feeling which should be created in us. We see bogies and imps of the cauldron, and pitchforks, and the little mosquito-like beings of the pantomimes, but we never see the God, the Spirit, which we ought to see; that is to say, the beautiful spirit, that patient, stern being who demands of a hero at least the heroic.

Shakespeare's characters are so often but weak beings; Lady Macbeth is perhaps the weakest of them all, and if that is the beauty—and unmistakably it is a great beauty—it is the beauty of disease and not the supreme beauty.

Having read of these characters, we are left to ourselves and our own contemplation, and each will add that thought which Shakespeare left to be added by each. There is great freedom permitted to the reader, for much has been left unsaid, but so much has also been said that nearly all is indicated, and to the imaginative brain these spirits are clearly implied and the fruits of the imagination are always welcomed by the unimaginative, who devour them as Eve must have devoured the forbidden fruit.

Therefore when a stage-manager happens to have imagination he must also set before the people the fruits of this imagination.

But look at the unwieldy material which is tossed to him! What can he do with rubbish such as scenery, such as costumes, such as moving figures which he can shove here and there and place in this or that light? Is this material for so subtle a thing as imagination to work with? Perhaps it is; perhaps it is no worse than marble or the material used for erecting a cathedral; perhaps all depends upon the manner of the use.

Well, then, admitting this, let the stage-manager return to the material and determine to shake the dust out of it until he wakens it to real life; that is to say, the life of the imagination. For there is only one real life in art, and that is this life of imagination. The imaginative, that is the real in art, and in no modern play do we see the truth of this so tremendously revealed as in *Macbeth*.

It is all very well for some people to talk about Shakespeare living in a curiously superstitious age, or choosing a theme from an age and a country which was soaked in superstition.

Good heavens! is the idea of a ghost, is the idea of a spirit, so strange? Why, then the whole of Shakespeare is strange and unnatural, and we should hastily burn most of his works, for we want nothing which can be called strange and unnatural in the twentieth century. We want something we can clearly understand, and, as represented upon the stage, these plays are not clear to understand, for the foolish appearance of a spook is not a very understandable thing, though the reality of the presence of spirits around us seems to me to be a thing which all ordinary intelligences should be reminded of.

Yet how can we show this thing properly if we take as the main and primary point for our consideration Macbeth and his wife, Banquo and his horse, and the thrones and the tables, and let these things blind us to the real issues of the drama?

Unless we see these spirits before we begin our work we shall never see them later on. For who can see a spirit by looking for it behind an act drop ? No, the man who would show these plays as Shakespeare, perhaps, might wish them to be shown must invest every particle of them with a sense of the spiritual; and to do so he must entirely avoid that which is material, merely rational, or rather, that which exposes only its material shell, for the beholder would then come up against something thick and impenetrable and have to return to that swinging rhythm which flows not only in the *words* of Shakespeare but in his very breath, in the sweet aroma which lingers round his plays.

But to speak more practically in conclusion.

Had I to teach a young man who would venture to achieve this I would act as follows: I would take him through each portion of the play, and from each act, each scene, each thought, action, or sound, I would extract some spirit, the spirit which is there. And on the faces of the actors, on their costumes, and on the scene, by the light, by line, by colour, by movement, voice and every means at our disposal, I would repeatedly and repeatedly bring upon the stage some reminder of the presence of these spirits, so that on the arrival of Banquo's ghost at the feast we should not commence to giggle, but should find it just and terrible; should be so keenly expectant, so attuned to the moment of its coming that we should be conscious of its presence even before we saw it there.

It would be the natural climax, the natural conclusion; and from that point until the end of the play I would remove spirit by spirit from the faces, from the dresses, from the scenes, until nothing lay upon the stage but the body of Macbeth, a handful of ashes left after the passage of a devouring fire.

By this means the scorn which the appearance of a spirit arouses in us would be averted; and before the public was aware of it, a spirit-world would once more become a possibility, our minds would again open to receive the revelation of the unseen; and we should feel the truth of Hamlet's words, "There are more things in heaven and earth, Horatio, than are dreamed of in your philosophy."

1910.

MACBETH

Here is a design for a scene which is in two parts.

The obvious question, always thoughtlessly put to me, is, whether people on the right of the theatre would see what was in the left-hand opening, and vice versâ.

It never occurs to some people that a theatre artist gives some of his time to making designs for modern theatre buildings—some of his time to designs for up-to-date buildings—and some of his time to buildings which sooner or later will be built. These people think an artist must be always " on the make."

This scene was made for a building which before long is sure to be erected.

I have even made some designs for buildings which mankind never will erect.

But surely there is time for all these things. It will help some one, if not myself, and it is surely still permitted to an artist to humour his fancy now and then.

I have also made designs for five or six different kinds of theatre buildings, and not merely designs but plans.

And I actually have the " impudence " to believe that these theatres will sooner or later all be tested by actual experiment. For what else have I worked?

[*Face page* 280.

SHAKESPEARE'S PLAYS

IN a little book, which I published in 1905,[1] I ventured to agree with those who hold the opinion that Shakespeare's plays were written for the Reader and not for the Stage. It seems many hold this opinion. Yet it was a satisfaction to me to come later across the following and other sentences in Goethe's writings—

"Shakespeare belongs by rights to the history of poetry; in the history of the Theatre he only appears casually."

"Shakespeare's whole method of proceeding is one which encounters a certain amount of impracticability upon the actual stage."

"The very contractedness of the stage forces him to circumscribe himself."

Goethe comes to this conclusion, not at the beginning of his life but at the end of it, after his experience in the theatre has shown him that literature and the stage are, and must be, independent one of the other. I still remain of the same opinion—that Shakespeare's plays are not for representation, more especially because I am myself now working on several Shakespearean representations, and therefore have occasion for passing in review the many different "editions," as they are called, of

[1] Reprinted here, p. 137.

Shakespeare, especially the stage editions, and I am struck by one fact, and it is this: that the people who hold that Shakespeare was a master of theatrical art cut away from these plays lines, passages—nay, whole scenes: these words, passages and scenes which, they say, were written for the stage.

To say a thing is perfect and then to mutilate it, is most peculiar. If a manager wishes to cut a play, saying it will be better understood by the public if he does so, it is permissible provided he does not at the same time say that Shakespeare was a perfect master of dramatic art. Drama is for the people if ever an art was for the people, and if Shakespeare has not made himself clear to the people of all time, the actor-manager is not going to improve matters by cutting out large portions of the text.

In *Hamlet* it is usual for that long passage commencing, "Now all occasions do inform against me," to be removed by the manager, who says that it does not "help the play." Now this is a most extraordinary state of affairs, that managers should be permitted to say what does or does not "help the plays" of Shakespeare, after Shakespeare has himself decided. Other passages in the play are removed because the managers hold that they are indelicate or they hold that the audience would consider them indelicate. Cut the passage between Ophelia and Hamlet in Act III, scene ii, when he is lying at her feet, and you rob the character of Hamlet of very much of its force. Ophelia, instead of being a woman of intelligence, becomes an early Victorian *débutante;* and Hamlet, instead of being a man of his time and suggesting a period which was more than a period of manners, becomes a kind of preaching curate.

Of course the Censor would object to this and other passages in Shakespeare, and he would be perfectly right, for the plays were not written for the stage; they were written to be read. If you wish to act them act them in their entirety or do not act them at all.[1] It is as ridiculous to say that the omission of a small passage is not going to harm such a work as to say that the omission of so small a portion of the body as the eye does not injure the whole.

This liberty with great plays is no sign of civilization; it is barbarous in the extreme. Another argument advanced for acting in this way is that the performance must not last longer than a certain time. Time has nothing to do with a performance. If it is good we do not mind how long it takes: if it is bad it must be cut short, and therefore to advocate a short time is to imply a fear on the part of the manager that the play is going to be badly

[1] ". . . I am very glad to find that I can endorse Tieck's opinion when he shows himself to be a zealous upholder of the unity, indivisibility, and unassailableness of Shakespeare's plays, and insists on their being performed in their entirety and without revision or modification of any kind."—GOETHE.

represented. Can one have too much of a good thing? Then, too, it is quite possible to perform a play of Shakespeare in its entirety in an evening provided the appliance for shifting the scenery is not so absurdly elaborate that it takes twenty minutes to change each act, and provided that the actors do not pause too long over each syllable, but exercise their brains to think a trifler faster. It is this slow delivery of Shakespeare's lines which has made Shakespeare a bore to so many people. Here in the plays of Shakespeare we have passionate scenes of an amazing description, far more amazing than in the plays of the south, and yet we drawl them and crawl them and are surprised when a Grasso comes to England and shows us how we should speak, act and reveal the suddenness and madness of passion. We seem to forget this fact, that passion is a kind of madness. We bring it to a logical attitude and we deliver it with the voice of the judge or the mathematician. It seems to have something to do with the totting up of accounts; thus with us it is a shopman, not Othello, who is throttling Desdemona. The emotional actors in England ought not to be content with themselves for not waking up and sweeping all these too deliberate and stodgy actors off the stage and out of the theatres.

Would the plays of Shakespeare be then interpreted as they should be? No, not even then. Not if the finest and most passionate actors in the world were to come together and attempt to perform Hamlet could the right representation of Hamlet be given, for I fear to represent *Hamlet* rightly is an impossibility.

1908.

REALISM AND THE ACTOR

YOU ask me if I consider Realism in acting to be a frank representation of human nature. Yes. Realism is exactly this : a frank representation of human nature. The modern writers and painters attest to this by *what* they write of and paint, and by the way in which they write and paint it.

And because the realists attempt to represent Nature so frankly (which frankness they call truth and which generally borders upon brutality), and because this frankness is no fruit, no blossom, but merely the roots of a new growth, so I believe that the actor will never ask for the same liberty as the writers and painters of to-day, that he may give these brutalities their " counterfeit presentment " with all accuracy of detail at command.

I can call to mind no actor so lacking in intelligence as to desire to present with all its actuality the moment of death as expressed by the modern realist in literature and painting, or the moments of love as expressed by these same frank and most, most blind leaders.

The realists may claim that they are not concerned so much with the subjects they treat of as with the manner in which they treat these subjects. If so, then, is it a most extraordinary fact that the realists only concern themselves with what is ugly or brutal, and always with what the idealists have given so much thought to *veil?*

The question you forgot to put me is whether the public would allow the actor to express the same feelings and the same incidents as both idealistic and realistic writers have somehow or other won the right to express.

What is the difference between the picture and the word, and the living, breathing actuality? Why, even the public that sits in the pit of a theatre feels the difference and would refuse to let the actor reveal what it allows Milton and Rabelais to reveal. Then how can there be a shadow of doubt that the actor not only should not be permitted the same liberty as the writer or painter, but actually *is not* permitted that licence?

Realism is a vulgar means of expression bestowed upon the blind. Thus we have the clear-sighted singing: "Beauty is Truth, Truth Beauty—that is all ye know on earth, and all ye need to know." The blind are heard croaking: "Beauty is Realism, Realism Beauty—that is all I know on earth, and all I care to know—don't cher know!"

The difference is all a matter of love. He who loves the earth sees beauty everywhere: he is a god transforming by knowledge the incomplete into the complete. He can heal the lame and the sick, can blow courage into the weary, and he can even learn how to make the blind see. The power has always been possessed by the artist, who, in my opinion, rules the earth.

It is quite likely that Realism may appeal at one

period to the public and not at another period. The public is not concerned with the quest of knowledge; no, not even with the wisdoms of wisdom, that simple everyday atom of truth which waits, unseen, everlastingly everywhere. The public is concerned with the quest of money—and, with money, that fat and brutal power to revenge which it can bring—that power to give like a lady a handshake when a kiss is too little; that power to give like a lord ten pounds to a "po'r beggah," and that power to give a little charity when only love is enough. And so long as the public is made up of this class of monstrous meanness, of that which gives half or three-quarters instead of all, so long will it love its Realism, which is the short measure or meanness of the artist.

Anyhow, there is nothing which need cause playgoers anxiety; there is no need for them to feel depressed; furious, if you like, but depressed? not a whit: for the limited section of playgoers who love beauty and detest Realism is a small minority of about six million souls. They are scattered here and there over the earth. They seldom, if ever, go to the modern theatre. That is why I love them, and intend to unite them.

Forte de' Marmi, 1908.

OPEN-AIR THEATRES

IT seems to me that the Theatre has nearly always longed to be "natural," that the playwrights, actors and scene-painters, have nearly always struggled to free themselves from being "theatrical." Even in the eighteenth century, when most things gloried in a sumptuous artificiality gorgeous in silver gilt, there appears a master who attempts to make all things "natural" again; and yet Molière's plays seem to us to-day anything but natural, and their ancient manner of representation strikes us as very artificial.

Not for one but for many centuries men have crowned their chosen playwright for that he was more "natural" than his fellows, yet the plays of Shakespeare no longer strike us as "natural"; even Robertson with his *Caste* and *Ours*, which were looked upon as very natural a few years ago, and their manner of representation quite like life, to-day seem antiquated, somewhat artificial.

There are some who go so far as to say that the earlier plays of Sir Arthur Pinero and the later plays by Mr. Shaw have grown artificial.

Scene-painting, too. A hundred years ago Clarkson Stanfield in England was painting scenery which amazed the critics by its "natural" appearance, and that, too, after they had known the work of de Loutherbourg; and soon Stanfield was looked on as unnatural, for Telbin the Elder gave them what they asserted was very Nature itself; and yet hardly have they said so before they eat their words, turn their backs on Telbin, and find true Nature in Hawes Craven, only to put him away a little later for Harker, who "at last paints Nature for us."

Nor is it any better with the acting. The Kembles and their grand artificiality had to make room for Edmund Kean, who in thirty years from then was looked on as anything but natural, for was not Macready "more natural"? And in a few years' time all of these actors seemed to us stilted and artificial when Henry Irving appeared. And now we talk of Irving's artificiality by the side of Antoine's natural acting. "It is Nature itself," cry the critics, and soon Antoine's natural acting is to become mere artifice by the side of the acting of Stanislawsky.

What, then, are all these manifestations of this "Nature"?

I find them one and all to be merely examples of a new artificiality—the artificiality of naturalism.

Dramatists, actors, scenic artists are under a spell—do you remember the story of the Sleeping Beauty?—and the spell must be broken before they can awake. To break it will be at once most hard and most easy—most hard to those who were born to sleep, most easy for one born to awaken; but most assuredly until this spell be *broken*, utterly and entirely destroyed, all the plays, acting and scenes on the stage of Europe must and will remain theatrical.[1]

I do not think the time has arrived when I can give you a hint of how to break this spell which lies over the European Theatre; besides, my purpose here is to put a question to you, not to answer one. It might be borne in mind that I have put my question to you without any thought of what is called its "practicality," and that the answers must be made in the same spirit. There is always a very natural desire in man (born of a sound caution) to keep things on a practical basis, and when we discuss economic or hygienic questions it is as well to be as practical as possible.

But where the question takes us outside that radius, and when we enter into discussion of those things which emanate from the spirit, such as the arts or philosophy, we might do well to consider them in as ideal a manner as they deserve; we can later on return to earth and attempt their symbolization. My question is this—

Do you feel that the Open-air Theatre is the right place in which to present the people with that

[1] Here we have to acknowledge that a certain charm (the very essence and reflection of that Romance which comes to us in Books . . .) lies in the pretty or swaggering artifice of the "theatrical." We most of us love the fun of the sham, and admire the playfulness of tinsel, powder and rouge; but all of us in the Theatre, from the first actor of the realm to the last call-boy of the provinces, are longing with all our hearts for the whole spirit of Nature to take possession of this, the home which we love.

which we call the Art of the Theatre, or do you feel that a roofed-in theatre is better? The first supplies us with natural conditions, the second with artificial conditions.

1909.

SYMBOLISM[1]

"IT IS IN AND THROUGH SYMBOLS THAT MAN, CONSCIOUSLY OR UNCONSCIOUSLY, LIVES, WORKS AND HAS HIS BEING: THOSE AGES, MOREOVER, ARE ACCOUNTED THE NOBLEST WHICH CAN THE BEST RECOGNIZE SYMBOLICAL WORTH, AND PRIZE IT HIGHEST."—CARLYLE.

SYMBOLISM is really quite proper; it is sane, orderly, and it is universally employed. It cannot be called theatrical if by theatrical we mean something flashy, yet it is the very essence of the Theatre if we are to include its art among the fine arts.

Symbolism is nothing to be afraid of—it is delicacy itself; it is understood as easily by the ploughman or sailor as by kings and other men in high places. Some there are who are afraid of symbolism, but it is difficult to discover why, and these persons sometimes grow very indignant and insinuate that the reason why they dislike symbolism is because there is something unhealthy and harmful about it. "We live in a realistic age," is the excuse they put forward. But they cannot explain how it is that they make use of symbols to tell us this, nor how it is that all their lives they have made use of this same thing which they find so incomprehensible.

For not only is Symbolism at the roots of all

1 "*Symbolism:* A systematic use of symbols; a symbol; a visible sign of an idea."—WEBSTER.

art, it is at the roots of all life, it is only by means of symbols that life becomes possible for us; we employ them all the time.

The letters of the alphabet are symbols, used daily by sociable races. The numerals are symbols, and chemistry and mathematics employ them. All the coins of the world are symbols, and business men rely upon them. The crown and the sceptre of the kings and the tiara of the popes are symbols. The works of poets and painters, of architects and sculptors, are full of symbolism; Chinese, Egyptian, Greek, Roman, and the modern artists since the time of Constantine have understood and valued the symbol. Music only became intelligible through the employment of symbols, and is symbolic in its essence. All forms of salutation and leave-taking are symbolic and employ symbols, and the last act of affection rendered to the dead is to erect a symbol over them.

I think there is no one who should quarrel with Symbolism—nor fear it.

1910.

THE EXQUISITE AND THE PRECIOUS

SWINE cannot appreciate pearls. This has at last become a well-known fact, acknowledged by the majority.

The majority of people known to us certainly appreciate pearls; therefore the majority may be said to appreciate that which is both exquisite and precious.

I do not care whether the pearls are appreciated because they are so rare and so costly—all the better that they are so—or because they look so lovely. Either reason is good enough, for the result is the same. Wonder and excitement are aroused, the things are sure to be handled tenderly, and the wearer will probably hold her head more charmingly than before. Thus we see that to be near the precious and the exquisite is to become more exquisite, more precious, ourselves.

It is a pity that the Theatre is neither exquisite nor precious.

I want, in place of violent expression of violent emotions and ideas, more exquisite expression of more precious emotions and ideas.

In place of vulgar materials, such as prose, coarse wooden boards, canvas, paint, *papier mâché* and powder, I would like more precious materials to be employed: Poetry, or even that far more precious Silence—ebony and ivory—silver and gold—the precious woods of rare trees—exquisite silks unusually dyed—marble and alabaster—and fine brains.

The public is no fool : it will not value a lump of coal above a diamond; it prefers silk and ivory any day to wood and canvas. A critic who denies this is a duffer.

So then, gentlemen, I ask you to consider the imitation Lily of the Theatre and to compare it with that more precious species, with her of the field.

And thanking you for past criticisms, I ask you to criticize justly the present material of the modern theatre. If you do so even with tolerance you will rouse us all to a state bordering upon exquisite rage; but you will confer upon the Theatre an honour—the honour of believing that it is still open to noble criticism, still worthy of judgment pronounced upon its essentials, and not alone upon its non-essential details.

If a fig-tree should bear thistles would you criticize the prickly result ? Would you waste your time protesting against the quality of the thistle and write it down an indifferent specimen and ask for better ?

Then why do you criticize the false product of our noble art ?

I pray you to study the Nature of the art of the Theatre, so that with your assistance once again the flower and fruit of it may be found to be both exquisite and precious.

1910.

Richard Clay & Sons, Limited, London and Bungay.

CPSIA information can be obtained at www.ICGtesting.com
Printed in the USA
BVOW03s0642230913

331841BV00004B/24/P

9 781290 936262